FLAGUPY

LITERATUR DER

ALBRECHT WIL

Dieser Katalog erscheint anläßlich der Ausstellung „Flagupy – Literatur der Armut“ im Literaturhaus Villa Clementine, Wiesbaden 31.8. bis 13.9.2013 und im Mainforum, IG Metall Hauptsitz, Frankfurt/M., 27.9. bis 19.10.2013.

ARMUT

Inhalt

Homeplus

„Jawohl, die Bank verkauft, was soll sie denn sonst machen?, und die Bank kauft zurück, weil es kein andrer tut, und die Bank kauft Sie, und die Bank kauft Sie aus und steuert Sie und steuert Sie wieder aus.“

ELFRIEDE JELINEK: Epilog zu: *Die Kontrakte des Kaufmanns, eine Wirtschaftskomödie,* 21.04.2009[1]

1 Zitiert nach http://www.elfriedejelinek.com/ (eingesehen am 27.06.2013).

Cover: Seoul, 2010 · Seite 1: Seoul, 2013 · Seite 4: Frankfurt/M., 2013 · Seite 5: Seoul, 2010

Flagupy – Literatur der Armut

Die Wortneuschöpfung „Flagupy" im Titel der Ausstellung formuliert eine Form des Protests in Anlehnung an die Occupy-Wallstreet-Bewegung.[2] Es ist ein Sprechakt mit aufforderndem Charakter: „To flag up" heißt übersetzt „die Flagge hissen". Interpretierend kann man darunter „Flagge zeigen" verstehen. Jelineks Drama mit dem Untertitel „Eine Wirtschaftskomödie" ist geeignet, einen Zugang zum Thema aufzuzeigen, denn Armut steht immer in Relation zum Reichtum von Gesellschaften. Armut betrifft seit den 1990er-Jahren zunehmend nicht nur ‚die Anderen' außerhalb Europas, sondern ist auch in Deutschland wieder verstärkt ein Thema.[3] Es handelt sich um neue Armutslagen in Deutschland, in denen die meisten Betroffenen zwar keinen Hunger leiden, jedoch zahlreichen gesellschaftlichen Exklusionen ausgesetzt sind. Am Gebäude der Villa Clementine in Wiesbaden hängen zwanzig überdimensionierte, auf Fahnenstoff gedruckte Bettelschilder, unterlegt von Nationalflaggen.[4] Die Flaggen verweisen auf die Herkunft der Bettelschilder und sie verdecken die Architektur aus der Gründerzeit teilweise. Die Kunstwerke ‚stören' damit den Anblick der repräsentativen Fassaden, wie es sonst nur Werbung an Gebäuden vermag. Wild zeigt Flagge:

> **„OBDACHLOS / Bitte um Spende/ Danke**
> [Wort doppelt unterstrichen, Anm. N. T.]"

lautet einer der Appelle und der Betrachtende fragt sich zu Recht, ob er etwas kaufen soll oder wer in der Gründerzeitvilla obdachlos sein könnte und ihn anbettelt. Was sich bei Albrecht Wilds Arbeiten entwickelt, ist in seiner Wirkung wenig vorhersehbar und genau dies ist beabsichtigt: Der Künstler arrangiert, doch die

---

2 Ich danke Katharina Menzel-Ahr (Ulm) für die kritische Diskussion dieses Beitrags.

3 Das vielverwendete Bild der sich öffnenden Schere zwischen Arm und Reich ist allerdings zu holzschnittartig. Es steigt die Ungleichheit der Einkommen in Deutschland. Dies ist nicht gleichbedeutend mit einer steigenden Armut. Vgl. KOLJA RUDZIO: *Armut. Steigt der Anteil der Armen in Deutschland? Viele glauben das, und die SPD will im Wahlkampf damit punkten. Doch es stimmt nicht,* in: DIE ZEIT, Nr. 52, 19.12.2012, S. 24; *Im Gespräch: Klaus Schroeder, Zeithistoriker an der Freien Universität Berlin. „Armutsforschung ist weitgehend politisch motiviert",* in: Frankfurter Allgemeine Zeitung, Nr. 298, 21.12.2012, S. 13.

4 Zum Literaturhaus in Wiesbaden vgl. KULTURAMT WIESBADEN (Hg.): *Das Literaturhaus Villa Clementine in Wiesbaden,* Regensburg 2009.

Objekte haben und entfalten ein Eigenleben, sie erzählen und visualisieren andere Leben und bilden im Ensemble ein vielstimmiges Werk, um das es im Folgenden gehen soll.

DAS FLOSS DER MEDUSA – ANFÄNGE IN LAUSANNE UND SEOUL

Albrecht Wilds Auseinandersetzung mit dem Thema Armut begann im Jahr 2006 mit einem Beitrag zum Ausstellungsprojekt Fluid Artcanal International. Die schwimmende Installation *Boatpeople* entstand in Zusammenarbeit mit der Künstlerin Suzanne Wild und bestand aus einer Floßkonstruktion, auf der bekleidete Schaufensterpuppen eine weiße Flagge hissen (Abb. 1). Die großen Plastiktüten, Wasserflaschen, eine männliche Figur im Tarnanzug mit einem Arm in der Schlinge und zwei verschleierte Frauenfiguren, eine davon liegend mit einer Babypuppe, lassen auf Kriegs- oder Bürgerkriegsflüchtlinge schließen. Das Floß war je drei Monate auf dem Canal de la Thielle in der Schweiz und anschließend dann auf dem Fluss Gapcheon in Daejeon (Südkorea) – also an Nicht-Kunstorten – unterwegs und erregte Irritation und Aufsehen.[5] Albrecht Wild verarbeitet das Ereignis zusätzlich in Form von Fotografien, in die er das Floß montiert. So entstehen Fotomontagen, in die er das Floß etwa vor der Kulisse von New York platziert, aufgenommen von der Fähre aus Staten Island kommend (Abb. 2). Wild erinnert damit an Einwanderer im 19. Jahrhundert aus Europa.[6] Die Kulisse von New York ist ein Sehnsuchtsort und Generationen von Einwanderern blickten aus dieser Perspektive auf New York. Man könnte allerdings auch an *Das Floß der Medusa* von Théodore Géricault denken.[7] Die Schiffbrüchigen der „Méduse“ erlangten eine schaurige Berühmtheit. Auf dem Floß aus Wrackteilen des während der Napoleonischen Befreiungskriege nach dem Senegal entsendeten Schiffes unter französischer Flagge brach nach Berichten von zwei Überlebenden Kannibalismus aus. Die Darstellung der Leichen und des Entsetzens, die mit den Konventionen des Historienbildes brach, führte zum Skandal, als das Werk 1819 im Pariser Salon ausgestellt wurde. Der Titel *Boatpeople*, ursprünglich eine Bezeichnung für die Bootsflüchtlinge des Vietnamkriegs, erinnert heute an Migrationswellen aus allen Teilen der Welt, vor allem an das Flüchtlingselend vor Lampedusa.

Abb. 1 Zusammen mit Suzanne Wild, Boatpeople, 2006/07, Installation, 240 × 225 × 290 cm, zerstört, © Foto: Christoph Stöh Grünig, Biel, Schweiz 2006

EINE SAMMLUNG VON BETTELSCHILDERN

Ausgangsmaterial für Albrecht Wild ist eine Sammlung von bislang mehr als zwanzig Bettelschildern, die vom Künstler dokumentiert wird. Zu jedem Schild

5 PETER JOCH (Hg.): *Albrecht Wild. I didn't expect this to happen to me ...*, Ausst.-Kat. IASK Changdong National Art Studio Seoul, Korea, National Museum of Contemporary Art, Korea 2008, S. 4–5.

6 Korrespondenz mit dem Künstler vom 23.06.2013.

7 THÉODORE GÉRICAULT, *Das Floß der Medusa*, 1818–1819, Öl auf Leinwand, 491 × 716 cm, Paris, Musée du Louvre. Vgl. ALBERT ALHADEFF: *The Raft of the Medusa. Géricault, Art, and Race*, München u. a. 2002.

Abb. 2 Boatpeople vor der Kulisse von New York, 2009, Fotomontage, 225 × 300 cm, Besitz des Künstlers

legt er eine Art Karteikarte an, die auf handschriftlichen tagebuchartigen Aufzeichnungen basiert und mit einem Bild versehen ist.[8] Diese Sammlung als Material und Nukleus für Kunst bedarf eines Kommentars zu ihrem Stellenwert im Werk von Albrecht Wild. Zuerst einmal kann festgehalten werden, dass es eine Sammlung und kein Archiv ist. Archivwürdig waren Aufzeichnungen aus Sicht der Archivare dann, wenn sie sich in eine spezifische Ordnung fügen.[9] Frühere Zeugnisse von Armen haben sich erhalten, weil sie im Austausch mit Behörden und Institutionen aufbewahrt wurden. Eine Sammlung von Schriftgut hingegen ist nach Ansicht der Archivpflege eine selektierte Ansammlung. Albrecht Wilds Sammlung versammelt Objekte und erinnert an Personen, mit denen er meist auch in Kontakt war. Die Bettelnden reagierten überrascht auf sein Anliegen, zuweilen galt es zu überzeugen, die Gegengabe des Künstlers beinhaltete neben einer Bezahlung eventuell auch das Schreiben eines neuen Schilds oder es kam nicht zum Verkauf. Mittlerweile sind auch andere Künstlerinnen und Künstler beteiligt, indem sie den Auftrag annehmen, aus anderen Ländern Schilder mitzubringen. Derzeit bilden die Reisebewegungen von Albrecht Wild und den beauftragten Künstlern die Mobilität und das Netzwerk des Künstlers ab: Frankfurt, Berlin, Paris, Wien, Budapest, Lissabon, Athen, New York, Kapstadt, Seoul u. a. Doch auch die Armen waren stets – meist nicht freiwillig – als Flüchtlinge bzw. Migranten mobil. Die gelegentlich unterlegten Flaggen der vergrößerten Bettelschilder bieten also keine verlässliche Orientierung hinsichtlich der Herkunft der Bettler. Armut wird allerdings statistisch sehr wohl zur nationalen wirtschaftlichen Angelegenheit und zum politischen Instrument, wie etwa der Armuts- und Reichtumsbericht der Bundesregierung oder unberechtigte nationalistische Ressentiments gegen Flüchtlinge beweisen.

Abb. 3 Ausstellungsansicht von *Pauvre Luxembourg* 2011 im Musée d'Histoire de la Ville de Luxembourg, © Foto: Julien Becker, Luxemburg

Auch die Sammlung der Bettelschilder wandert, aufbewahrt in einem Reisekoffer. Dieser Koffer dient als Vehikel, wenn etwa der Künstler als Kurier Werke für eine Ausstellung in ein Museum bringt. Waren sie einmal Arbeitsinstrumente für Bettelnde, so stellen die Schilder im Museum, in einer Kirche oder im Atelier Verschiedenes dar: Es sind Erinnerungen, Objekte, Leihgaben und Autographen. Selbst wenn nur die Originalschilder ausgestellt werden wie in der Luxemburger Ausstellung *Pauvre Luxembourg* 2011 ist der Kontextwandel entscheidend (Abb. 3).[10] Der Ausstel-

8 Grundlage dieses Beitrags sind die zwanzig Bettelschilder, die für die Wiesbadener Ausstellung auf Banner gedruckt wurden.

9 Mario Wimmers brillante Studie zur Entstehung des Selbstverständnisses der Archivwissenschaft als eine Archäologie der Sprache des Archivs im 19. Jahrhundert betont die klare Abgrenzung zwischen Archiv und Sammlung aus Sicht der Archivare. Vgl. MARIO WIMMER: *Archivkörper. Eine Geschichte historischer Einbildungskraft,* Konstanz 2012, S. 51.

10 MARIE-PAULE JUNGBLUT/CLAUDE WEY (Hg.): *Armes Luxemburg? Pauvre Luxembourg?,* Ausst.-Kat. Musée d'Histoire de la Ville de Luxembourg, München 2011, S. 310–313.

lungsraum und die an Schmuckvitrinen erinnernde Form der Vitrinen ‚veredeln' die Bettelschilder und sind ein Beispiel dafür, dass die vieldiskutierte Präsentation einer Sammlung im Galerieraum, dem sogenannten White Cube, keinesfalls eine Neutralisierung der Objekte zur Folge hat. Denn Bettelschilder behalten zwar ihren appellativen Charakter, doch werden sie durch die Präsentationsform neu konnotiert.

BETTELSCHILDER ALS LITERATUR DER ARMUT

Bettelschilder können als eine Form von Gebrauchsliteratur betrachtet werden, die Konventionen folgt.[11] Aus Sicht von Historikern sind Bettelschilder ‚Armutszeugnisse' und Ego-Dokumente, die in den letzten Jahren in den Blickpunkt rückten, weil sie individuelle Lebenslagen von Armut darstellen.[12] Während Institutionen und Bürokratien der Armenfürsorge gut dokumentiert sind, interessieren Selbstzeugnisse von Armen in Form von politischen Kampagnen erst in jüngerer Zeit, als zum Beispiel *Voices of Poverty* des European Anti Poverty Network (EAPN) das Augenmerk auf das arme Individuum lenkte, das aus dem Kollektiv heraustritt.[13] Albrecht Wilds Werke sind vor diesem Hintergrund auch als eine Art Stimmensammlung zu betrachten. In globalisierten Verhältnissen mit migrierenden Bildern, reisenden Künstlern und wandernden Armen interagieren diese Werke weltweit – wobei diese Interaktion überwiegend von Kunstschaffenden und Kuratorinnen und Kuratoren gesucht wird. Dennoch unterscheiden sich die Texte voneinander und in manchen Ländern gibt es sehr wohl Armut, aber keine Bettelschilder. So ist es etwa in Japan undenkbar, dass Bettelschilder geschrieben werden und auf diese Weise Spenden zu erbitten.[14] Ich bezeichne die Texte im Folgenden als eine Stimmensammlung, weil viele dem Sprachstil der gesprochenen Sprache entsprechen, was auch für ältere Ego-Dokumente zutrifft, weshalb der Historiker Thomas Sokoll empfiehlt, Bittschriften und Briefe laut zu lesen.[15]

Abb. 4 Bettelschild, New York City, Wellpappe, erworben 2009 in New York, Besitz des Künstlers, © Foto: Sook Jin-Jo, New York City

11 Zum Thema Ökonomie, Arbeit und Literatur vgl. u. a. ELKE BRÜNS (Hg.): *Ökonomien der Arbeit. Soziale Verhältnisse in der Literatur,* München 2008; FRANZISKA SCHÖSSLER (Hg.): *Arm und Reich in der Literatur,* in: Der Deutschunterricht. Beiträge zu seiner Praxis und wissenschaftlichen Grundlegung, Jg. 64/2012, H. 5; NICOLE COLIN/FRANZISKA SCHÖSSLER (Hg.): *Das nennen Sie Arbeit? Der Produktivitätsdiskurs und seine Ausschlüsse,* Heidelberg 2013.

12 So sind etwa die Bittschriften und Petitionen von Armen aus England gut erschlossen. Vgl. THOMAS SOKOLL: *Selbstverständliche Armut: Armenbriefe in England, 1750–1850,* in: WINFRIED SCHULZE (Hg.): Ego-Dokumente. Annäherungen an den Menschen in der Geschichte, Berlin 1996 (Selbstzeugnisse der Neuzeit, 2), S. 227–271. Vgl. für den deutschen Sprachraum u. a. AGNES SCZESNY: *Der lange Weg in die Fuggerei – Augsburger Armenbriefe des 19. Jahrhunderts,* Augsburg 2012; PETER HINTZEN: *„Da ich mir selbst nicht helfen kann". Arme und Armenfürsorge in der zweiten Hälfte des 19. Jahrhunderts, dargestellt im Spiegel der Armenbriefe der Bürgermeister Deutz 1846–1888,* Dissertation Universität Trier 2013.

13 Vgl. http://www.eapn.eu/en/news-and-publications/publications/eapn-books/eapn-book-voices-from-the-poverty-line-jobs-and-unemployment-in-the-eu (eingesehen am 25.06.2013).

14 Gespräch mit Albrecht Wild am 18.05.2013.

15 THOMAS SOKOLL: *Writing Relief. Rethoric in English Pauper Letters, 1800–1834,* in: ANDREAS GESTRICH/STEVEN KING/LUTZ RAPHAEL (Hg.): *Being Poor in Modern Europe. Historical Perspectives*

Das Bettelschild des Vietnamveterans Walt gab Albrecht Wild die Idee zur Kombination von Bettelschildern mit Nationalflaggen, da Walt sein Schild mit der amerikanischen Flagge schmückte. 2009 erwarb es die Künstlerin Sook Jin-Jo in New York für Albrecht Wild (Abb. 4):

> **„Vietnam 63-71 8 YRS US.M.C.** [US Marine Corps, Anm. N.T.] **/ HOMELESS VET. / WITH FAMILY + SM. CHILDREN / PLEASE HELP / ANYKIND OF DON. / HAVENT WORKED IN 3 YRS.** [in der rechten unteren Ecke:] **THANK YOU WALT“**

Wir erfahren in platzsparend abgekürzten Wörtern, dass Walt von 1963 bis 1971 im Vietnamkrieg bei den Marines gedient hat und dass er eine Familie mit kleinen Kindern hat. Seit drei Jahren ohne feste Arbeit, ist ihm jede Art von Zuwendung willkommen. Aus größerer Distanz weniger gut lesbar sind weitere Zusätze in den oberen Ecken. Entzifferbar ist oben rechts: „67-US / KHE SAHN“. Walt war demnach 1967 in der vietnamesischen Stadt Khe Sanh, wo sich die Khe Sanh Combat Base der Marines befand.[16] Entscheidend ist, dass folgende Worte aus der Entfernung gut lesbar sind: „homeless vet.“, „with family“, „please help“ und „anykind of don.“. Die am Schild befestigte Flagge unterstützt den patriotischen Appell an die Mildtätigkeit der Passanten. Wenn das Schild in Wiesbaden als Banner am Gebäude der Villa Clementine hängt, liefert das Werk durch die Neukontextualisierung einen Kommentar: Die Stimme von Walt wird erhöht und die ungleiche Beziehung zwischen Spender und Empfänger wird umgekehrt. Der potentielle Spender blickt zur Frieszone des Gebäudes auf und wird von oben – also aus der üblichen Geberperspektive – mit der Botschaft des Schilds konfrontiert. Als „aus dem Augenwinkel – right in your face“ wurde Wilds Vorgehen in einer früheren Ausstellung bereits charakterisiert.[17]

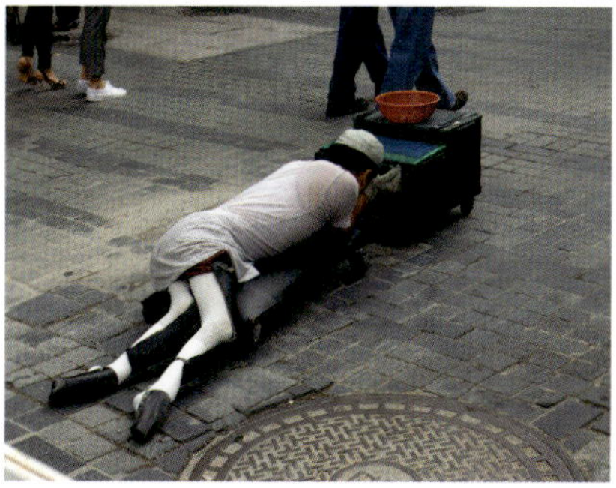

Abb. 5 Bettler auf der Straße Insadong in Seoul (Südkorea), 2009, Fotografie, Besitz des Künstlers

NEUE FORMEN DES BETTELNS

Es handelt sich bei den Bettelschildern um Gebrauchsliteratur mit einer appellativen Funktion, die meist auf Wellpappe geschrieben wird. Ihre Materialität ist bedeutsam, also auch die Gebrauchsspuren.[18] Ähnlich wie bei einem Spendenplakat gilt es, die Aufmerksamkeit des Passanten zu erhalten, doch muss ein bestimmter Grad an Unprofessionalität gewahrt bleiben, um nicht in Verdacht zu geraten, kein bedürftiger Gabenempfänger zu sein. Wie professionell darf ein Schild aus-

1800–1940, Bern 2006, S. 91–111, S. 109.

16 In der linken oberen Ecke finden sich genauere Angaben zu Dienstzeiten in der Armee: „I Tour / WBI / 6 NOV- / 2 MAR. / 33R[?] / Trops / NAM[?]N“; oben rechts: „67- US / KHE / SAHN / 3 RBMBR / 5 BRTT“.

17 KunstKulturKirche Allerheiligen/Andreas Wörsdörfer (Hg.): ALBRECHT WILD: *„… aus dem Augenwinkel – RIGHT IN YOUR FACE“*, Ausst.-Kat. KunstKulturKirche Allerheiligen / Forum für Moderne Kunst und Neue Musik, Frankfurt/M. 2010.

18 So enthalten einige der Bettelschilder Spuren ihrer Besitzer in Form von Fingerabdrücken oder Haaren.

sehen, um noch glaubhaft zu sein? Und in welchen Fällen ist ein direkter Kontakt zwischen Spender und Empfänger der Gabe noch erforderlich? Warum werden in Europa keine Visitenkarten mit Bettelschildern akzeptiert oder LED-Displays mit Übersetzungen in mehreren Sprachen? Diese Fragen stellte sich Wild während seines Aufenthaltes in Seoul 2007/2008, einer Stadt, in der Reich und Arm mit unvermittelter Härte aufeinander treffen (Abb. 5). Die zahlreichen in Südkorea entstandenen Fotografien zeigen auch die Gleichgültigkeit von Passanten, die mit diesen Formen von Armut und Elend vertraut sind.
So schlängelt sich ein gelähmter Bettler auf einem Brett mit Rollen vorwärts durch die Insadong, eine Straße in Seoul. Er schiebt dabei einen gepolsterten Kasten auf Rollen vor sich her, auf dem die Spendenschale steht. Auffallend sind die Handschuhe, die Kopfbedeckung und die weiße Strumpfhose, so dass anders als bei den vorbeilaufenden Passanten kaum nackte Haut zu sehen ist. Neben den Bettelschildern bilden diese Fotografien bewegender Gegensätze zwischen Arm und Reich in der Metropole Seoul eine weitere Sammlung im Werk von Albrecht Wild: Sie ist zum Teil dokumentarischer Art und kann als Erinnerungsstütze weitere Werke anregen. Doch ebenso können die Fotografien für sich stehen.

Auf die eingangs gestellte Frage, wie professionell ein Bettelschild sein darf, antwortete Albrecht Wild künstlerisch. Bannerwerbung und flimmernde Displays erheischen heutzutage kurzfristig Aufmerksamkeit in der Großstadt, so dass die Methode des Bettelns mit handgeschriebenen Schildern nicht mehr zeitgemäß erscheint. Albrecht Wilds Kunstprojekte zu Formen des Bettelns überschreiten Grenzen, indem er die handgeschriebenen Schilder in Konkurrenz zu einer Welt der gedruckten und digitalisierten Form von Werbung setzt. Daraus resultieren Wilds Weiterentwicklungen des Bettelns in Form von Visitenkarten mit aufgedruckten Bettelschildern, Ansteckbuttons in Bonbonfarben und Bettelschilder als Bannerwerbung, die er in die urbanen Settings von Seoul integrierte (Abb. 6, 7). Dabei geht es ihm darum, die Professionalisierung des Bettelns konsequent weiterzuentwickeln, ohne die darin liegende Widersprüchlichkeit zu kommentieren. Diese Diskussion ist Aufgabe des Betrachters, eine Rollenverteilung, die an gesellschaftskritische Kunst der 1960er- und 1970er-Jahre erinnert. Konsequent ist die Digitalisierung des Bettelschilds in Form eines LED-Displays zum Umhängen (Abb. 8). Damit verbindet Wild Technologie und Betteln, um den urbanen Raum zu bespielen. Die sich bewegende Laufschrift ermöglicht dauernd wechselnde Schriftbilder und sie passt sich dem jeweiligen Umfeld an, indem die Texte in verschiedenen Sprachen eingegeben werden können.

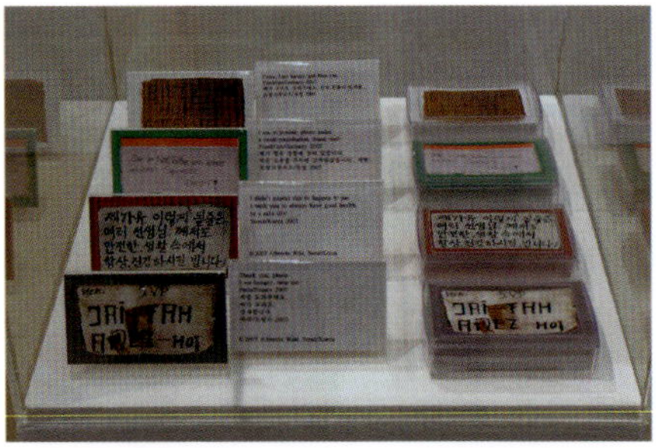

Abb. 6: Business-Cards, 2007

Abb. 7: Nahe City Hall in Seoul, 2007, fiktive Werbekampagne, Fotomontage

Andere Künstler haben Bettelautomaten als eine neue Kunstform des Bettelns entwickelt. Bettelautomaten in der Kunst entstehen als Antwort auf Bettelverbote, mit denen Bettler aus dem Stadtbild eliminiert werden sollen. Stellvertretend sei der Bettelautomat von Kaspar J. König genannt, der nach Bettel-

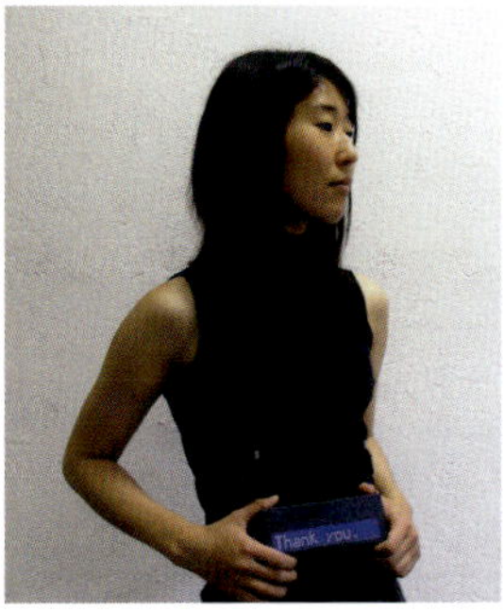

Abb. 8: LED-Display zum Umhängen, getragen von der Künstlerin Zero Reiko Ishihara, 2009

verboten in Fußgängerzonen in Slowenien entstand.[19] Das konsequente Ersetzen des Menschen provoziert Widerspruch. So veranlasste das Bettelverbot in der Steiermark im Jahr 2011 die Kuratoren Michael Behr und Astrid Kury zur Ausstellung *Wir sind Bettler*, die gegen das politisch gewollte Verschwinden der Bettler im Stadtbild von Graz künstlerisch argumentierte.[20] Ein gezeigter Bettelautomat von zweintopf aus dem Jahr 2008 etwa schafft Distanz zu Bettelnden, indem diese nur via Fernsehbildschirm, der auf einen Einkaufswagen montiert ist, virtuell anwesend sind.

Diesen Kunstaktionen, die sich in gesellschaftspolitische Debatten einmischen, steht Wilds Kunst thematisch nahe. Jedoch geht es Wild nicht um das Ersetzen des Menschen durch Automaten, sondern um Digitalisierung als zeitgemäßes Hilfsmittel des Bettelns. Dabei schließen sich eine Anpassung an die veränderten Bedingungen des Bettelns und eine künstlerische Überformung nicht aus.[21]

TEXT UND BILD

Es handelt sich bei den in Wiesbaden ausgestellten, auf Flaggenstoff aus Polyestergewebe gedruckten Bettelschildern um „Schriftbilder"[22], denn jede für den Betrachter lesbare Schrift trägt eine doppelte Dynamik in sich. Neben der Präsenz des Schriftkörpers – zum Beispiel seine graphische Gestaltung – gibt es die Repräsentationsfunktion des Zeichens, indem der Vorgang des Sehens und sofortigen Lesens der Schrift wiederum Bilder hervorbringt.[23] Betrachten wir solche Texte zunächst als Literatur und erst in einem zweiten Schritt als Bilder.
Die Texte sind meist in einem einfachen Sprachstil verfasst. Sie bestehen zuweilen auch nur aus unvollständigen Sätzen: „Bin in Not, bitte um eine / kleine Spende / Danke!" (Kat.-Nr. 9). Manche der Schilder aus Europa enthalten eine Referenz zur christlichen Mildtätigkeit:

„BITTE ICH-HABE / HUNGER / GOTTES-SEGEN"

stellt Gottes Lohn in Aussicht und steht damit in der Tradition der christlichen Karitas und der Werke der Barmherzigkeit, wobei Mildtätigkeit auch ein Bestandteil anderer Religionen ist wie etwa die Zakat im Islam und die Zedakah im Ju-

19 Vgl. *Armes Luxemburg?* (wie Anm. 10), S. 308-309; siehe auch den Kurzfilm zum Objekt: http://www.youtube.com/watch?v=fgz4Zmx4nkk (eingesehen am 20.06.2013).

20 Vgl. die Kooperationsausstellung von der Akademie Graz und dem Stadtmuseum Graz im Stadtmuseum Graz vom 14.04.2011–04.06.2011. Ich danke Astrid Kury für die Zusendung der unveröffentlichten Dokumentation der Ausstellung.

21 Vgl. hierzu *Instant Housing* von Winfried Baumann, Vehikel für Obdachlose, die auch von Hilfsorganisationen erworben werden können. Vgl. HERBERT UERLINGS/NINA TRAUTH/LUKAS CLEMENS (Hg.): *Armut – Perspektiven in Kunst und Gesellschaft,* Ausst.-Kat. Stadtmuseum Simeonstift/Rheinisches Landesmuseum Trier/Stadtmuseum Ulm, Darmstadt 2011, S. 399, Kat.-Nr. 151 (Nina Trauth).

22 Vgl. zum Schriftbild die Überlegungen von SUSANNE STRÄTLING/GEORG WITTE: *Einleitung,* in: dies. (Hg.): *Die Sichtbarkeit der Schrift zwischen Evidenz, Phänomenalität und Ikonizität,* München 2006, S. 7–20.

23 Ebd., S. 9.

dentum.[24] Eine Stimme eines Bettelschilds aus Seoul spricht: „Ich hätte nicht gedacht, dass mir das passieren könnte ... Ich wünsche Dir ewige Gesundheit in einem guten Leben." Beide Texte enden mit einer rhetorischen Wunschformel für den potentiellen Spender, der an europäische Bettelliteratur des 19. Jahrhunderts erinnert. So endet etwa die 1824 verfasste Petition von Ann Marsh mit den Worten: „She [Ann Marsh, Anm. N. T.] will ever acknowledge with grateful thanks to her kind benefactors".[25]

Untersucht man die verwendeten Wortfelder, so gibt es ungeachtet der Nationalität wiederkehrende Topoi. Es sind Hunger und Krankheit sowie Arbeitslosigkeit und daraus resultierende Obdachlosigkeit. Als weitere Gründe für die Not werden Kinderreichtum und Schulden genannt. Die Stimmen unterscheiden sich dabei deutlich in ihrem Stil. Manche wenden sich an den Spender mit einer Anrede, wie sie in einer Rede üblich ist: „Sehr geehrtes Publikum"[26] oder wie in einer Kleinanzeige: „Suche!", wie Sven es tut.[27] Nur manche nennen ihren Namen. Auch die Gabe, um die gebeten wird, differiert. So ist es in der Regel nur eine kleine Spende, es ist das Kleingeld oder eine Essensmarke, worum wir gebeten werden, und nicht mehr. Dafür genügen wenige Worte:

> **„Merci S. VP / JAI-FAM** [sic] **/ AIDEZ-MOI"**
> (Danke Bitte / Ich habe Hunger / Helfen Sie mir). [28]

Mit dem Dank zu Beginn wird dabei die übliche Ordnung von Anrede, Mittelteil und Schluss gebrochen. An diesem Beispiel wird deutlich, dass der Text nicht der gewohnten Leserichtung folgen muss. Darüber hinaus funktioniert er situativ: Die Art und Weise wie „Danke" und „Bitte" eventuell mit einem Blickkontakt unterstrichen werden, entscheidet, ob es zu einer Spende kommt. Mit der Wahl der Sprache ist es auch möglich, bestimmte Personenkreise anzusprechen. So wird Englisch verwendet, um sich an Touristen zu wenden, Sprachen wie das Arabische hingegen sind an Landsleute gerichtet (Kat.-Nr. 17). Auch haben die Stimmen ein Geschlecht: Frauen benennen Kinderreichtum als Grund für ihre Armut.

Insgesamt offenbaren die Schilder mittels konventioneller Topoi Biografien, die im Text um der Spende willen ausgebreitet werden. Es ist ein Akt der Selbstoffenbarung, zu dem der Bettelnde im öffentlichen Raum genötigt wird. Selbstoffenbarung, wie zum Beispiel auch in manchen Fernsehformaten des Privatfernsehens, ist ein zweischneidiges Schwert und im Fall des Bettelnden folgt ihr nicht automatisch eine Anerkennung, da er auf seine Armut oder Arbeitslosigkeit reduziert wird. In Albrecht Wilds Werk bleibt die Anonymität der Autorinnen und Autoren gewahrt. Wir lesen ihre Texte und interessieren uns auf diese Weise

---

24 Vgl. die Schlüsselbegriffe „Zakat" von Tonia Schüller und „Zedakah" und „Gemilut Chassadim" von Rainer Josef Barzen sowie ders.: *Jüdische Armenfürsorge. „Ich, der Herr, schaffe Gnade, Recht und Gerechtigkeit"* und SARAH VANESSA LOSEGO: *Sozialfürsorge für französische Muslime 1945–1965,* in: UERLINGS/TRAUTH/CLEMENS: *Armut* (wie Anm. 21), S. 66–67, S. 82–91 und S. 311–317.

25 Wahrscheinlich wurde die Petition an die Verantwortlichen der Pfarrgemeinde von Chelmsford in Essex von Charles Loosey of Long Alley im Auftrag von Ann Marsh verfasst. Vgl. THOMAS SOKOLL: *Writing Relief* (wie Anm. 15), S. 97–99.

26 Bettelschild Lissabon, 2011, Kat.-Nr. 4.

27 Bettelschild, Frankfurt 2013, Kat.-Nr. 13.

28 Bettelschild, Paris 2007, Kat.-Nr. 15.

für die Schicksale, ohne deren Porträts zu kennen, was ungewöhnlich ist in einer Welt, die zunehmend visuell, vor allem über Bilder rezipiert wird.

DER TEXT ALS BILD

Eine Textanalyse von Bettelschildern, ohne das Schriftbild zu berücksichtigen, wäre unvollständig. Der bereits zitierte Text „Merci / S. VP / JAI-FAM [sic] / AIDEZ-MOI (Danke Bitte / Ich habe Hunger / Helfen Sie mir) entfaltet seine Wirkung auch durch das Schriftbild: Das „Danke" und das abgekürzte „Bitte" sind kleiner geschrieben, wahrscheinlich später hinzugefügt worden, um den Appell „Bitte helfen Sie mir" zu steigern. Entscheidend ist auch, wie der Raum gefüllt wird. Es sind keine ausgeprägten Handschriften, da die bevorzugten Versalien den Fluss der Schrift häufig unterbrechen. Das auf Fernwirkung ausgelegte Schriftbild wird mit breitem, meist dunklem Filzstiftstrich erzeugt. Die Großbuchstaben gilt es zu füllen. Dabei wird die Horizontale der Zeilen entweder strikt eingehalten, so dass der Eindruck eines Druckbilds entsteht, oder schwingend gebrochen.[29] Selten wird der Raum frei genutzt, wie zum Beispiel auf dem Bettelschild aus Kapstadt (Kat.-Nr. 6). Die Form des Schilds aus gerissenem Karton mit seitlichen Grifföffnungen für die Hände gibt den Schwung der Schrift vor, die diagonal geführt ist und deren Versalien mit Schraffur gefüllt werden. Insgesamt dominiert bei den handgeschriebenen Bettelschildern die Orientierung am Druckbild von Gebrauchsgrafik und gedruckter Werbung. Selten werden farbige Abbildungen ausgeschnitten und auf die Kartons aufgeklebt (Kat.-Nr. 3). Das Heiligenbild zeigt zwei kniende Frauen zur Linken und einen Schäfer mit Schaf zur Rechten. Die Gläubigen schauen zu einer erhöhten Figur auf, von der nur die Schuhe und ein Teil des weißen Kleids noch sichtbar sind, weil der obere Teil der Darstellung fehlt. Ikonographisch könnte es sich sowohl um eine Anbetung Mariens als auch Jesu handeln.[30] Mit dem Heiligenbild wird eine Andachtssituation geschaffen. Das Bild verstärkt die Botschaft, dass die Frau krank sei und fünf Kinder habe. Die Stimme spricht:

> **„Ich kann nicht arbeiten. Wir danken Ihnen für eine Cabe!** [sic]**".**

Auf diese Weise werden die Knienden auf dem Heiligenbild zu den Empfängern der Gabe und die Leserinnen und Leser zur christlichen Nächstenliebe animiert. Solche Heiligenbilder erinnern auch an Devotionalien und Dankesgaben von geheilten Kranken an Wallfahrtsorten.

Insgesamt sind die Bettelschilder auch Bildträger, indem die Verfasser die Schrift innerhalb des rechteckigen Schildes graphisch anordnen, ihre Texte unterzeichnen oder Bilder in die Darstellung integrieren.

VON CARTELLE UND SCHILDERN

Geht man der Frage nach, seit wann es Bettelschilder gibt und wie der Diskurs zwischen Spender und Empfänger verschriftlicht worden ist, so begibt man sich

29 Bettelschild, Frankfurt/M., Flohmarkt 2007, Kat.-Nr. 10.

30 Eine Himmelfahrt Christi ist wegen des Bildausschnitts naheliegend. Allerdings wäre eine Himmelfahrt, bei der Christus Schuhwerk trägt, ikonographisch ungewöhnlich.

auf die Spuren einer Geschichte der Literatur der Armut, die hier nur angerissen werden kann. Sie ist untrennbar mit der Geschichte der Bildung und Alphabetisierung verknüpft. So konnten und können viele Arme nicht lesen und schreiben. Zudem überwiegen die Zeugnisse der Besitzenden bis heute auch deswegen, weil sie als sammlungswürdig galten.

Im Spiegel der griechischen antiken Dramenliteratur war der Bettler Objekt des Spotts und der Belustigung.[31] Eindeutig abwertend ist auch ein in Pompeji erhaltenes Graffito mit dem Schriftzug „Abomino paupero[s]" (Ich verabscheue Arme).[32] Vor dem Hintergrund der Antike ist das religiöse Konzept der Karitas revolutionär. Zuvor hatte es in Europa keine religiös formulierte Notwendigkeit für das Almosen gegeben. Viele Bettlerdarstellungen im Mittelalter und der Frühen Neuzeit sind Teil der Repräsentation der Armenfürsorge aus Sicht der Kirche oder der Stadt als Auftraggeber.[33] Interessant ist in allen Darstellungen das gemalte Verhältnis von Spender und Empfänger der Gabe.[34] Löchrige und flickenbesetzte Kleidung, Verkrüppelung, die Bettlerschale oder die geöffnete Hand sowie Bettelstab und Löffel kennzeichnen den Bettler der Frühen Neuzeit in der Malerei und Graphik.[35] Man denke etwa an *Die sieben Werke der Barmherzigkeit* von Pieter Brueghel d. J.[36] Heute werden Arme zuweilen mit Bettelschild oder Bettelschale stilisiert, weil Armut in westlichen Industriegesellschaften ohne solche Attribute nicht mehr eindeutig erkennbar ist. Jogginganzüge und Turnschuhe etwa sind mittlerweile World Fashion und kein eindeutiges Zeichen für Armut.

Schriftstücke spielen in einigen Gemälden der Frühen Neuzeit eine wichtige Rolle. Eine der berühmtesten Darstellungen ist Juseppe Riberas *Der Junge mit dem Klumpfuß* (1642), der an der Krücke einen Zettel befestigt hat mit der Aufschrift „Da mihi elimo / sinam propter amorem Die" (Gib mir ein Almosen für die Liebe Gottes).[37] Doch schrieb dies wohl nicht der Junge, der wahrscheinlich nicht schreiben konnte. Schrifttäfelchen, ital. „cartelle", sind in Gemälden ein Kommunikationsmittel zwischen Betrachter, Maler und Auftraggeber – nicht das

31 PETER KRUMBACH: *Schauspieler und Darsteller in der antiken Gesellschaft*, in: STEPHAN SEILER (Hg.): *Armut in der Antike. Perspektiven in Kunst und Gesellschaft*, Ausst.-Kat. Rheinisches Landesmuseum Trier 2011, S. 53–56, S. 55.

32 Zitiert nach STEPHAN SEILER (Hg.): *Armut in der Antike. Perspektiven in Kunst und Gesellschaft*, Ausst.-Kat. Rheinisches Landesmuseum Trier 2011, S. 8.

33 Bettlerdarstellungen der Frühen Neuzeit in Freskenprogrammen von Hospitälern und Kirchen sind positiv konnotiert, während die Druckgraphik und Literatur wie das *Liber Vagatorum* nördlich der Alpen Bettler zu Gaunern stigmatisiert. Vgl. dazu TOM NICHOLS: *Irony and Ideal in Sixteenth-Century Beggar Imaginary*, Manchester u. a. 2007, S. 6.

34 Vgl. PHILINE HELAS: *Repräsentation der Wohltätigkeit. Der Akt des Gebens und Nehmens im Bild zwischen dem 13.–20. Jahrhundert*, in: LUTZ RAPHAEL/HERBERT UERLINGS (Hg.): *Zwischen Ausschluss und Solidarität. Modi der Inklusion/Exklusion von Fremden und Armen in Europa seit der Spätantike*, Frankfurt/M. u. a. 2008, S. 37–63.

35 Vgl. hierzu zuerst ELISABETH SUDECK: *Bettlerdarstellungen vom Ende des XV. Jahrhunderts bis zu Rembrandt*, Straßburg 1931.

36 PIETER BRUEGHEL D. J., *Die sieben Werke der Barmherzigkeit*, zwischen 1616 und 1638, Öl auf Holz, 43,3 × 57 cm, Ulm, Museum der Brotkultur. Vgl. UERLINGS/TRAUTH/CLEMENS: *Armut* (wie Anm. 21), S. 359, Kat.-Nr. 50.

37 MICHAEL SCHOLZ-HÄNSEL: *Jusepe de Riberas „Der Junge mit dem Klumpfuß" (1642) als Schlüsselwerk der Armenikonographie im Kontext von Konfessionalisierung und Disziplinierung*, in: ANDREAS GESTRICH/LUTZ RAPHAEL (Hg.): *Inklusion/Exklusion. Studien zur Fremdheit und Armut von der Antike bis zur Gegenwart*, 2. Aufl. Frankfurt u. a. 2008, S. 451–478, S. 461.

der Armen. Es sind Diskurse um die richtige Konfession und um Armenfürsorgepolitik zwischen Kirche und Staat. Betteln zu dürfen, erforderte eine Genehmigung, weshalb Bettler Bettelbriefe oder Bettelmarken mit sich führten, die ihnen das Betteln erlaubte. Fehlten die Papiere oder wurde deren Fälschung entdeckt, so landeten sie im Gefängnis.[38]

Sucht man im Grimm'schen Wörterbuch das Wort „Bettelschild", so findet man es noch nicht. Stattdessen sind es Begriffe wie „Bettelbrief", „Bettelschelle", „Bettelvisite" und „Bettelliedlein".[39] Das Wortfeld verrät, dass die Formen des Bettelns im deutschen Sprachraum nicht stumm waren. Bettelmusikanten benötigten keine Schilder. Solche sind auf dokumentarischen Fotografien der 1930er-Jahre zu sehen, als Menschen infolge der Weltwirtschaftskrise mit Schildern arbeitssuchend an Straßenecken standen.[40] Mit dem Verfügbarwerden des Materials Wellpappe als Verpackungsmaterial für Lebensmittel wurden Kartons aus Wellpappe zum objet trouvé, aus dem Bettelschilder und provisorische Behausungen bis heute entstehen.[41] Das lautstark vorgetragene Betteln verstummte im 20. Jahrhundert zumindest in Europa, als auch Werbung und Reklameschilder in den Städten Einzug hielt.[42]

Abb. 9 Jani Leinonen: Anything helps, 2005–2009, 22 gerahmte Bettelschilder, 53. Biennale, Dänischer Pavillon, Venedig, © Foto: courtesy of Jani Leinonen

ANYTHING HELPS? – BETTELSCHILDER IN DER ZEITGENÖSSISCHEN KUNST

Seit den 1990er Jahren beschäftigen sich immer mehr Künstlerinnen und Künstler mit Fragen der Ökonomie, der Gerechtigkeit und des Stellenwerts von Arbeit im 21. Jahrhundert und seiner gesellschaftspolitischen Dimension.[43] Das Projekt *Anything helps* des finnischen Künstlers Jani Leinonen unterscheidet sich in wesentlichen Punkten von dem Ansinnen Albrecht Wilds, obwohl Leinonen ebenfalls mit Bettelschildern arbeitet und so auch über moderne Formen des Bettelns nachdenkt.[44] Vorgestellt seien hier die während der Biennale 2009 im

38 Vgl. UERLINGS/TRAUTH/CLEMENS: *Armut* (wie Anm. 21), S. 377, Kat.-Nr. 96 (Nina Trauth).

39 JACOB UND WILHELM GRIMM: *„Bettelbrief", „Bettelliedlein", „Bettelschelle" und „Bettelvisite"*, in: dies.: *Deutsches Wörterbuch*, 16 Bde. in 32 Teilbänden, Leipzig 1854–1961 und 1971 (Quellenverzeichnis), Bd. 1, Sp. 1727, 1729, 1731, 1733, http://woerterbuchnetz.de/DWB/?sigle=DWB&mode=Vernetzung&lemid=GB05986 (eingesehen am 12.06.2013).

40 Vgl. etwa eine arbeitslose Stenotypistin mit einem Schild, aufgenommen im Jahr 1930. MATTHIAS REISS: *Zwischen Revolte und Resignation. Das Bild des Arbeitslosen seit dem 19. Jahrhundert*, in: UERLINGS/TRAUTH/CLEMENS: *Armut* (wie Anm. 21), S. 326–335, S. 333, Abb. 220.

41 Wellpappe für die Verpackung von Waren wurde Ende des 19. Jahrhunderts in den USA patentiert und die erste europäische Wellpappenfabrik wurde 1883 gegründet. Vgl. HEINZ SCHMIDT-BACHEM: *Aus Papier. Eine Kultur- und Wirtschaftsgeschichte der Papier verarbeitenden Industrie in Deutschland*, Berlin. 2011, S. 680–682. Vgl. zum Karton als Material für provisorische Behausungen von Obdachlosen auch den Ausst.-Kat. *Einrichten. Leben im Karton*, bearb. v. Petra Oelschlägel, Ausst.-Kat. Städtische Galerie Villa Zanders, Bergisch-Gladbach 2008.

42 Ob es eine Relation gibt oder ob es sich um eine zufällige Koinzidenz handelt, bleibt zu untersuchen.

43 Vgl. FRANZISKA EISSNER/MICHAEL SCHOLZ-HÄNSEL (Hg.): *Armut in der Kunst der Moderne*, Marburg 2011.

44 Vgl. DANIEL BIRNBAUM (Hg.): *Making Worlds – Venedig, Biennale 53rd International Art Exhibition*,

Dänischen Pavillon ausgestellten Bettelschilder, da die Präsentation in Venedig die Aussagen der Kunstobjekte ebenfalls entscheidend veränderte (Abb. 9).[45] Der Dänische und der Nordische Pavillon wurden von den Künstlern Michael Elmgreen und Ingar Dragset kuratiert, die die Ausstellungsgebäude als Wohnhäuser zweier fiktiver Privatsammler interpretierten, weshalb die kuratorische Arbeit den Titel „The Collectors" trägt.[46] Leinonens Arbeit besteht aus 22 mit Goldrahmen versehenen Bettelschildern, die in Vierer- und Fünferblöcken übereinander die Esszimmerwand schmückten. Die Städte, aus denen die Schilder stammen, werden auf einer Messingplakette auf dem Glas benannt. Auf der Homepage des Künstlers wird *Anything helps* zum Monument der Schuld und Klassendifferenz erklärt und mit einer Spendenaktion verknüpft.[47] Leinonen positioniert sich nicht als mahnender Beobachter, er ist ein Teil des Gesamtsystems: „I want to get rid of class distinction but all I think and do is a result of class distinction".[48] Obwohl das Ausgangsmaterial das Gleiche ist, bleibt im Gegensatz dazu bei Albrecht Wild die Person des Künstlers im Hintergrund. Er begleitet, dokumentiert und kontrolliert die Rezeption seiner Arbeiten nicht mit der Homepage als einer Form der Selbstdarstellung. Es geht in Wilds Werk in der Tradition der Konzeptkunst um die Suche nach neuen künstlerischen Ausdrucksformen, die auf andere Weise Kritik üben und Protest bekunden.[49] Allerdings wird bei der Interpretation in beiden Fällen die Kontextualisierung bedeutsam: In Venedig werden Bettelschilder in Goldrahmen sammlungswürdig, in der Luxemburger Armutsausstellung von Albrecht Wilds Werken wurde dies mittels der Vitrinen geleistet. Um stärker auf die Literatur der Armut zu fokussieren, wählte Wild für die Wiesbadener Ausstellung die Banner im Außenraum.

FLAGGENKUNST – FLAGUPY

Die Nationalflagge als Bildträger für Bettelschilder ist eine besondere Art der Rahmung. Sie konfrontiert mit einer Kartographierung der Welt nach Ländern. So signalisiert das Unterlegen eines Motivs mit der Flagge einen nationalen Zusammenhang, den Hinweis auf ein Territorium bzw. auf ein erinnerungswürdiges Monument, bekannt durch Darstellungen von Nationaldenkmälern etwa auf Post-

---

Venedig 2009, Bd. 2, S. 26–31, S. 30. Die Arbeit in Venedig ist nicht identisch mit der Edition *Anything helps™ 10 % of Your Purchase Goes to the Poor (Germany Edition)* von Plastikschildern nach originalen Bettelschildern, die in Vilnius gezeigt wurde, obwohl Jani Leinonen zu dieser Zeit Bettlerschilder zu sammeln begann (Korrespondenz mit Jani Leinonen, 27.06.2013. Vgl. zu der 2005 ausgestellten Arbeit PAUL SCHMELZER: *New, improved Beggar Signs* (09.10.2005), in: http://eyeteeth.blogspot.de/2005/09/new-improved-beggar-signs.html (eingesehen am 10.06.2013); PERNILLE ALBRETHSEN u. a.: *Notes on Works and Projects*, in: LARS BANG LARSEN/CRISTINA RICUPERO/NICOLAUS SCHAFHAUSEN (Hg.): The Populism Catalogue, Ausst.-Kat. The Contemporary Art Centre, Vilnius/National Museum of Art, Architecture and Design, Oslo/Stedelijk Museum, Amsterdam/Frankfurter Kunstverein, Berlin/New York 2005, S. 23–31, S. 27–28, Abb. S. 106.

45 Leinonen erwarb 2003 das erste Bettelschild aus Texas, das den Titel gab.

46 PETER WEIBEL/ANDREAS F. BEITIN (Hg.), *Elmgreen & Dragset. Celebrity – The One and the Many*, Ausst.-Kat. Zentrum für Kunst- und Medientechnologie, Karlsruhe, Köln 2011, S. 207–254, S. 250.

47 Siehe http://janileinonen.com/en/ (eingesehen am 05.06.2013).

48 Ebd.

49 Einordnung von PETER JOCH, in: *Albrecht Wild. I didn't expect this to happen to me …*, (Anm. 5), S. 16.

karten.[50] Den Bettelschildern – als solche bleiben sie als aufgedrucktes Objekt erkennbar – kommt mit dieser passepartoutartigen Rahmung eine Bedeutung zu, die zum Hinsehen auffordert. Sind mit den Flaggen affirmative wie kritische Diskurse des Nationalismus und Patriotismus verknüpft, so thematisieren die Texte Obdachlosigkeit, die sich einer Zuordnung zur Flagge widersetzt. Die Schilder lassen sich zwar mit der Nationalflagge des Landes unterlegen, in dem sie erworben wurden. Sie verweisen damit jedoch mitnichten auf die jeweilige Nationalität der Bettelschildbesitzer.

Patriotische, kritische und andere Verwendungen von Nationalflaggen in der Kunstgeschichte haben eine lange Tradition. Im 20. Jahrhundert etwa ist es die exzessive Bearbeitung der amerikanischen Flagge im Werk von Jasper Johns, in der Flagge und Gemälde ununterscheidbar werden. Claes Oldenburg collagierte die amerikanische Flagge aus brauner Wellpappe in patriotischer Absicht.[51] Die Flagge als Markierung von Territorium und Grenze sowie deren Verschiebungen thematisierte Alighiero Boetti in seiner Wandteppichserie *Mappa*. Seine Weltkarten visualisieren die einzelnen Staaten in den Farben der jeweiligen Nationalflaggen.[52] Durch die nationale Einfärbung der Bettelschilder fokussiert Albrecht Wild ebenfalls auf Land, Besitz und Grenze, was in Kombination mit den Stimmen der Armen irritiert und deshalb zielführend ist: Dieses Nationalitätenprinzip war und ist bei den mobilen Armen, wie bereits erwähnt, fragwürdig, aber politisch bedeutsam, denn die Mobilität der Armen war und ist nicht grenzenlos. Sie wird von Staaten durch Aufnahmeregelungen gesteuert und spätestens bei der statistischen Quantifizierung wird das Länderprinzip wirksam. Es entsteht ein Wettbewerb im internationalen Vergleich, um den Milleniumsentwicklungszielen der Vereinten Nationen nachzukommen oder um Arme vom eigenen Staatsgebiet fernzuhalten, indem Flüchtlinge nach der Drittstaatenregelung bzw. nach dem Dubliner Übereinkommen in Europa nicht aufgenommen werden. Das irritierende Moment der Nationalflagge in Kombination mit dem gedruckten Bettelschild ist Wilds künstlerischer Beitrag zur gesellschaftlichen Diskussion. Der Künstler vertraut auf das ästhetische Potential der Texte, deren Hilferufe die repräsentative Funktion der Flaggen konterkariert. Es ist ein widerständiger Kommentar, nach Aussagen des Künstlers ist er auch durchaus „boshaft" gemeint.

Abb. 10: Simulation mit Bettelschildern am Stadtmuseum Simeonstift Trier, 2011, Fotomontage

50 Vgl. DANIEL HOHRATH (Hg.): *Farben der Geschichte. Fahnen und Flaggen. Aus den Sammlungen des Deutschen Historischen Museums*, Ausst.-Kat. Deutsches Historisches Museum, Berlin 2007.

51 CLAES OLDENBURG, *Big Cardboard Flag*, 1960, 57,2 × 96,5 ×3,8 cm, Tinte auf Wellpappe auf Holz, Privatsammlung (Christie's New York, 16.11.2006). Die Flagge soll an die Landnahme der ersten amerikanischen Siedler in Provincetown erinnern, wo sich der Künstler 1960 aufhielt. Vgl. ACHIM HOCHDÖRFER: *Von der „Street" zum „Store". Claes Oldenburgs Pop Expressionismus*, in: ders. (Hg.): *Claes Oldenburg. The Sixties*, Ausst.-Kat. Musum Ludwig, Köln u. a., Wien 2012, S. 12–71, Abb. S. 35, S. 38.

52 Vgl. EVA SCHARRER/ANDREA VILIANI: *Alighiero Boetti*, in: EVA SCHARRER/KATRIN SAUERLÄNDER: *Documenta 13. Das Begleitbuch*, Bd. 3, Ostfildern 2012, S. 46, Kat.-Nr. 30.

SIMULATIONSKUNST UND WIRKLICHKEIT: DIE HÄNGUNG DER BANNER IM ÖFFENTLICHEN SAKRALEN UND POLITISCHEN RAUM

Abb. 11 Simulation mit Bettelschildern im Innenhof des IG-Metallhauses in Frankfurt/M., 2013, Fotomontage

Als Vorarbeit zum nun realisierten Projekt in Wiesbaden und Frankfurt kann eine Simulation am Stadtmuseum Simeonstift in Trier gelten (Abb. 10). Die Montagen sind Hilfsmittel, um Projekte zu simulieren, zu verwirklichen oder zu erinnern. Bei den Vorarbeiten für die Trierer Ausstellung *Armut – Perspektiven in Kunst und Gesellschaft* im Jahr 2011 entstand eine solche Montage für den Innenhof des Stadtmuseums Simeonstift Trier, ein Projekt, das nicht verwirklicht wurde. Die historische Örtlichkeit des Simeonstifts, das um 1140 gegründet wurde, besteht aus einem fast quadratischen Vierflügelbau, neben der bis zur Säkularisierung als Stiftskirche genutzten Porta Nigra. Die Anbringung von Bettelschildern an diesem ehemals geistlichen Ort hätte eine enge inhaltliche Verbindung zu dem Namenspatron aufgewiesen. Der Grieche Simeon ließ sich als Einsiedler in den Ostturm der Porta Nigra einsperren und lebte dort in freiwilliger Armut. Bald nach seinem Tod 1035 wurde er heiliggesprochen, der römische Torbau zur Doppelkirche über dem Grab Simons umgebaut und ein Kanonikerstift gegründet.[53] Nicht alle Schilder sind mit einer Nationalflagge unterlegt und die Banner passen sich nicht in den Rhythmus der Arkadengliederung ein, sondern sie bilden einen Fries, der durch die unterlegten Farben zum Fremdkörper auf der historischen Architektur wird. Ein Vergleich mit der Simulation des Innenhofs des IG Metall-Gebäudes verdeutlicht, dass die Architektur und Örtlichkeit die Wirkung der Arbeiten mit bestimmt (Abb. 11). So ist die Assoziation mit Bannerwerbung bei der modernen Architektur stärker gegeben, sie unterstützt die Arbeit der Industriegewerkschaft Metall und integriert sich in Kampagnen der Gewerkschaften im Kampf um faire Arbeitsbedingungen und Bezahlung. Die Mitglieder der Vereinten Dienstleistungsgemeinschaft (Verdi), nach der IG Metall zweitgrößte Gewerkschaft im Gewerkschaftsbund, bemächtigen sich beim Kampf gegen Lohndumping ebenfalls provokativ der Literatur der Armut. So war kürzlich auf einem Schild der Demonstranten in Frankfurt zu lesen: „Hey Boss, haste mal 'nen ... [Euro, Anm. N.T.]".[54] Im Arbeitskampf um Tariferhöhungen wird die Praxis des Bettelns als eine Art von Satire aufgeführt, um Lohnerhöhungen zu erreichen.

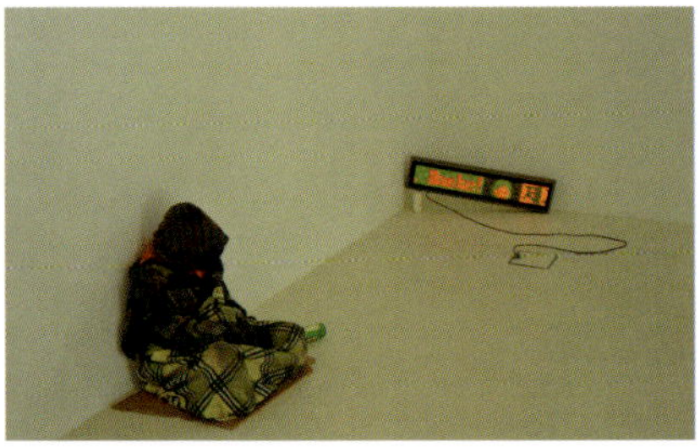

Abb. 12 Sitzender, 2008, verschiedene Materialien, 70 × 70 × 55 cm, Besitz des Künstlers, © Foto: Bernhard Matthias Lutz, Trier

Die Collage am Simeonstift wird hingegen stärker als Fremdkörper wahrgenommen. Realisiert wurde schließlich ein Sitzender in Kombination mit einem LED-Display mit Literatur der Armut als einen Schlusspunkt im zweiten Obergeschoss der Ausstellung (Abb. 12).[55] Dort kam es zu Störungen des Gewohnten in der Art, dass die Besucher des Museums auf das Kunstwerk reagierten, indem sie

53 ELISABETH DÜHR/FRANK G. HIRSCHMANN/CHRISTL LEHNERT-LEVEN (Hg.): *Stadtgeschichte im Stadtmuseum. Begleitband zur neuen stadtgeschichtlichen Ausstellung im Stadtmuseum Simeonstift Trier*, Trier 2007, S. 35–37.

54 Dc. Berlin: *Handel wehrt sich gegen Vorwurf des Lohndumpings*, in: Frankfurter Allgemeine Zeitung, Nr. 134, 13.06.2013, Pressefotografie von Bernd Kammerer, S. 11.

55 UERLINGS/TRAUTH/CLEMENS: *Armut* (wie Anm. 21), S. 400, Kat.-Nr. 153–154 (Nina Trauth).

die übliche Rolle des Spenders einnahmen und der Figur Geld gaben. Das Spenden wiederholte sich während der gesamten Ausstellungszeit.

In der Frankfurter Allerheiligenkirche wurde 2010 eine direkte Gegenüberstellung von Bannern und einer sitzenden Figur realisiert, wobei die Bettelschilder durch eine plane Hängung an der Wand stärker an Plakate erinnern (Abb. 13). Die Figur im rechten Kirchenschiff folgt nicht der bereits erläuterten geläufigen Bettlerikonographie mit abgerissener Kleidung und Spendenschale, sie verbirgt darüber hinaus ihr Gesicht und hockt auf dem Steinboden der Kirche. Erst wenn die Figur und die Literatur der Armut zusammen gelesen werden, erschließt sich die sitzende Figur. Der sakrale Raum fördert stärker noch als der Kunstraum eine Verwechslung des Kunstwerks mit einem realen Menschen. So wurde Wilds Installation von Kirchgängern aufgefordert, Platz zu nehmen. Die Verantwortlichen wollten deshalb – wie die Besucher der Trierer Armutsausstellung – diese Uneindeutigkeit durch eine Spendenschale beseitigen und Wilds Installation eindeutig als ‚Armutskunst' mit Appellcharakter vereinfachen.

DIE KUNST DER KRITIK

Abschließend sei ein Resümee gezogen, um die Gedankengänge dieses Essays zusammenzuführen. Die Bettelschilder Albrecht Wilds sind eine Sammlung besonderer Art mit einem Künstler als Sammler, Kurator und Zeugen. Doch sind diese Schilder nicht das Kunstwerk selbst, sondern sprechendes Material. Für Albrecht Wild sind Bettelschilder eine zu sammelnde Form der Literatur der Armut. Aus Bettelschildern und Fotografien als einer Art Gedächtnis und Erinnerung entstehen Installationen mit dreidimensionalen Bildern von sitzenden und liegenden Körpern. Die Banner mit den Bettelschildern sind also nur ein Teil der Auseinandersetzungen mit den Formen des Bettelns und dem künstlerischen Material. Albrecht Wilds Arbeiten geben Anstöße, das Thema Armut auf eine neue Weise wahrzunehmen und andere Perspektiven einzunehmen. Doch seine der Konzeptkunst nahestehende Kunst erschöpft sich darin nicht. Es geht dem Künstler nicht vorrangig um Aktionismus im Sinne einer einfachen propagandistischen Botschaft *gegen* Armut, worauf Kunst, die sich des Themas Armut annimmt, häufig reduziert wird. Dabei besteht nicht nur bei seinem Werk die Gefahr, Offenheit und Ambivalenzen auf eine Story zu reduzieren.

Abb. 13 Die Kauernde, 2010, verschiedene Materialien, 60 × 43 × 78 cm, Besitz des Künstlers (Installation in der Allerheiligenkirche in Frankfurt/M.)

Spezifisch für sein Vorgehen ist die Überführung in neue Kontexte, so dass bei seiner ‚sozialen' Kunst an Nicht-Kunstorten die Grenzen zwischen Werk, Betrachter und Umgebung sich verunklären und ein Handeln im sozialen Raum hervorbringen, das ein Teil des Werks wird. Dies ist zwar dem Phänomen Armut geschuldet, jedoch auch der Handschrift des Künstlers, die erst auf den zweiten Blick sichtbar wird: Albrecht Wild gestaltet und initiiert den gesellschaftlichen Raum. Dabei verzichtet er auf eine eindeutige Story, wie zum Beispiel gängige Medienformate und appellative Kunst gegen Armut sie formulieren, und vertraut dem ästhetischen Potential der Literatur der Armut. Falls Wiesbadens Presse als Reaktion auf das mit Bannern behängte Literaturhaus titeln würde: „Stadt im

Aufruhr"[56] – dann wäre Wilds Werk ein Auslöser dafür. Das störende Potential mit einfachen Mitteln ist eine Form ‚sozialer' Kunst, die ästhetisch und gesellschaftspolitisch parallel zu den geläufigen Mediendiskursen und visuellen Repräsentationen agiert – ähnlich den Occupy-Bewegungen. Der Störfaktor Kunst ist eine Möglichkeit, um Kritik zu üben. Kritik sei hier nach Michel Foucault verstanden als eine „Kunst der freiwilligen Unknechtschaft, der reflektierten Unfügsamkeit".[57] Sie wendet sich gegen eine Bevormundung durch staatliche und mediale Autoritäten, die beim Thema Betteln einen Kanon ‚politisch korrekter' Darstellungsformen wiederholen oder das Betteln verbieten.

POSTSKRIPTUM

Wenige Jahre, bevor die Villa Clementine erbaut wurde, war es in Wiesbaden 1873 zu einem Brotkrawall gekommen, ein Wort, das heute nicht mehr in Gebrauch ist. Denn Hungerrevolten sind in Deutschland historisch geworden.[58] Das Wort „Krawall", entstanden in der Zeit des Vormärz zwischen 1815 und 1848, beinhaltet lautmalerisch den Aufruhr.[59] Allerdings ging der Wiesbadener Brotkrawall über einen lautstarken Protest gegen angeblich hohe Brotpreise hinaus. Backsteinmacher, Handwerksgesellen und Dienstboten kämpften im prosperierenden Wiesbaden der Gründerzeit gegen die staatliche Autorität und für faire Löhne.[60] Solche Protestformen standen damals ebenso unter Strafe wie das Betteln. So schreibt Hugo von Strauß, Polizeidirektor von Wiesbaden, im Jahr 1874: „Die Bettelei lässt bis jetzt, trotz angestrengtester Fahndung, nicht nach."[61] Die Ausstellung der Werke von Albrecht Wild im 21. Jahrhundert erinnert an diese Ereignisse, obwohl die Geschichte des Ortes nicht die Idee zur Installation gab. Im Gegensatz zu früheren Zeiten ist es nun eine visuelle Form des Krawalls, der Aufmerksamkeit erregt.

56 Beitrag zum Festival „Maximierung Mensch" des Theaters Trier, vgl. www.tufa-trier.de/veranstaltungen/detailansicht/article/Stadt-in-Aufruhr.html (eingesehen am 15.06.2013).

57 Diese Formen von Kritik reagieren auf eine zunehmende Bevormundung von Individuen, bewirkt durch eine Bündelung von Praktiken, die der französische Philosoph Michel Foucault als Gouvernementalität bezeichnet hat. Foucault führt dazu aus: „Wenn es sich bei der Regierungsintensivierung darum handelt, in einer sozialen Praxis die Individuen zu unterwerfen – und zwar durch Machtmechanismen, die sich auf Wahrheit berufen, dann würde ich sagen, ist die Kritik die Bewegung, in welcher sich das Subjekt das Recht herausnimmt, die Wahrheit auf ihre Machteffekte hin zu befragen und die Macht auf ihre Wahrheitsdiskurse hin. Dann ist die Kritik die Kunst der freiwilligen Unknechtschaft, der reflektierten Unfügsamkeit. In dem Spiel, das man die Politik der Wahrheit nennen könnte, hätte die Kritik die Funktion der Entunterwerfung.", zitiert nach MICHEL FOUCAULT: *Was ist Kritik?*, übersetzt von Walter Seitter, Berlin 1992, S. 15.

58 HORST STEFFENS: *Der Wiesbadener Brotkrawall von 1873. Ursachen und Hintergründe sozialer Protestbewegungen in den frühen 1870er Jahren*, in: Nassauische Annalen. Jahrbuch des Vereins für nassauische Altertumskunde und Geschichtsforschung 100 (1989), S. 175–196.

59 JACOB UND WILHELM GRIMM: „Krawall", in: dies.: Deutsches Wörterbuch, 16 Bde. in 32 Teilbänden, Leipzig 1854–1961 und 1971 (Quellenverzeichnis), Bd. 11, Sp. 2125–2127, Sp. 2125, http://woerterbuchnetz.de/DWB/?sigle=DWB&mode=Vernetzung&lemid=GK13019 (eingesehen am 12.06.2013).

60 STEFFENS: *Der Wiesbadener Brotkrawall* (wie Anm. 58), S. 185.

61 Ebd., S. 190.

FLAGGEN

Folgende Doppelseite: Installationsidee an der Fassade der
Villa Clementine, Wiesbaden (Eingang und Nordfassade). Fotomontage

KÉREM SEGITSENEK
EGY GYEREKEM VA
MAGUK SEGEDÉLI
NÉLKÜL ÉHEZNEK
KÖSZÖNÖM SZÉPE
Suche!
Arbeit und eine Wohnung!
Danke!
Sven!
سبحان الله
بفضل اعانتكم
انني عائش
شكر لكم

HABE 2 KINDER ZU VERSORGEN
UND HOHE SCHULDEN.
BITTE UM EINE KLEINE
SPENDE. VIELEN DANK!
Bin in Not bitte um eine
kleine Spende
DANKE!
VIETNAM
HOMELESS VET.
PLEASE HELP
SORRY ANY
Job please help
me
I have got nothing
please

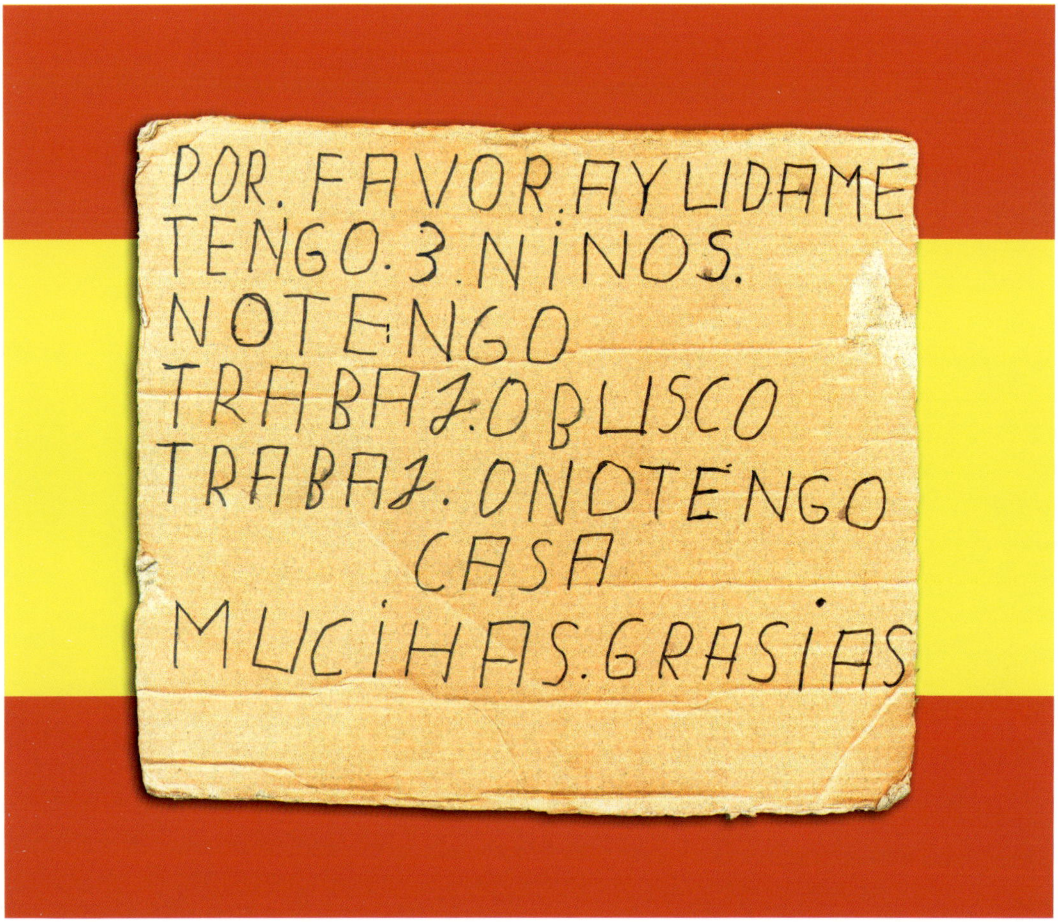
POR. FAVOR.AYUDAME
TENGO.3.NINOS.
NOTENGO
TRABAJ.OBUSCO
TRABAJ.ONOTENGO
CASA
MUCIHAS.GRASIAS

Kat.-Nr. 1

Kat.-Nr. 2

ICH BIN KRANK
OPERIERT, HABE 5
KINDER UND SIEHABEN
HUNGER. ICH KANN NICHT
ARBEITEN, WIR DANKEN
IHNEN FÜR EINE GABE!
DANKE.

Kat.-Nr. 3

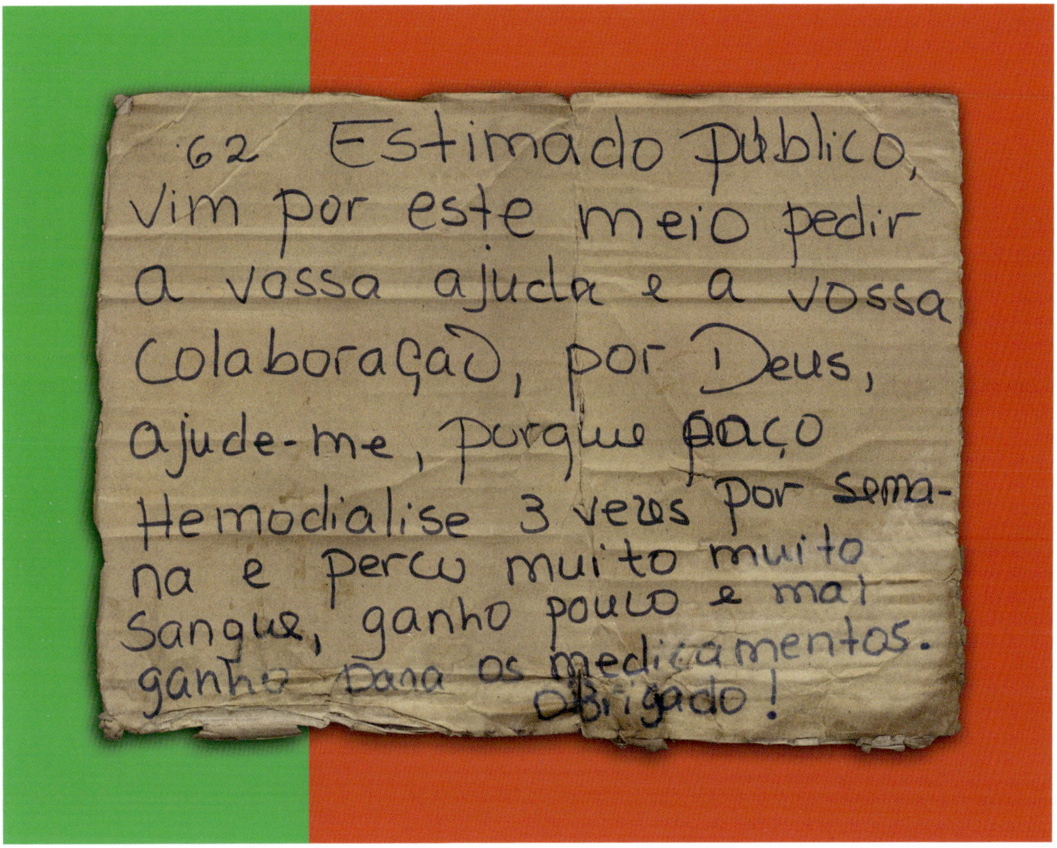
62 Estimado público,
vim por este meio pedir
a vossa ajuda e a vossa
colaboração, por Deus,
ajude-me, porque faço
Hemodialise 3 vezes por sema-
na e perco muito muito
sangue, ganho pouco e mal
ganho para os medicamentos.
Obrigado!

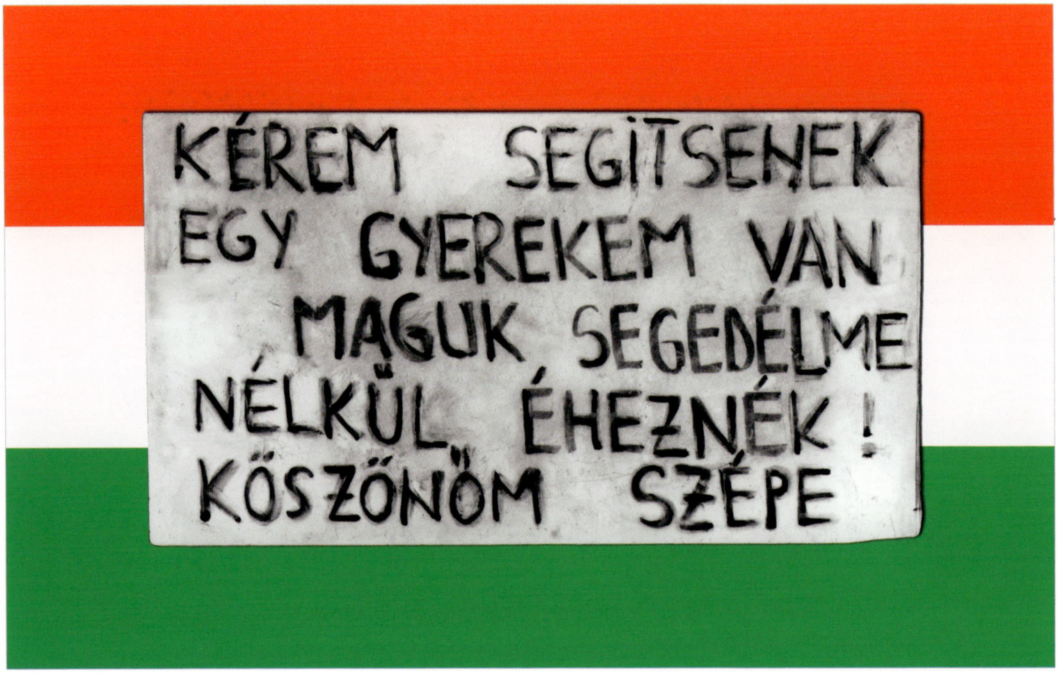
KÉREM SEGİTSENEK
EGY GYEREKEM VAN
MAGUK SEGEDÉLME
NÉLKÜL ÉHEZNÉK!
KÖSZÖNÖM SZÉPE

Kat.-Nr. 5

Kat.-Nr. 6

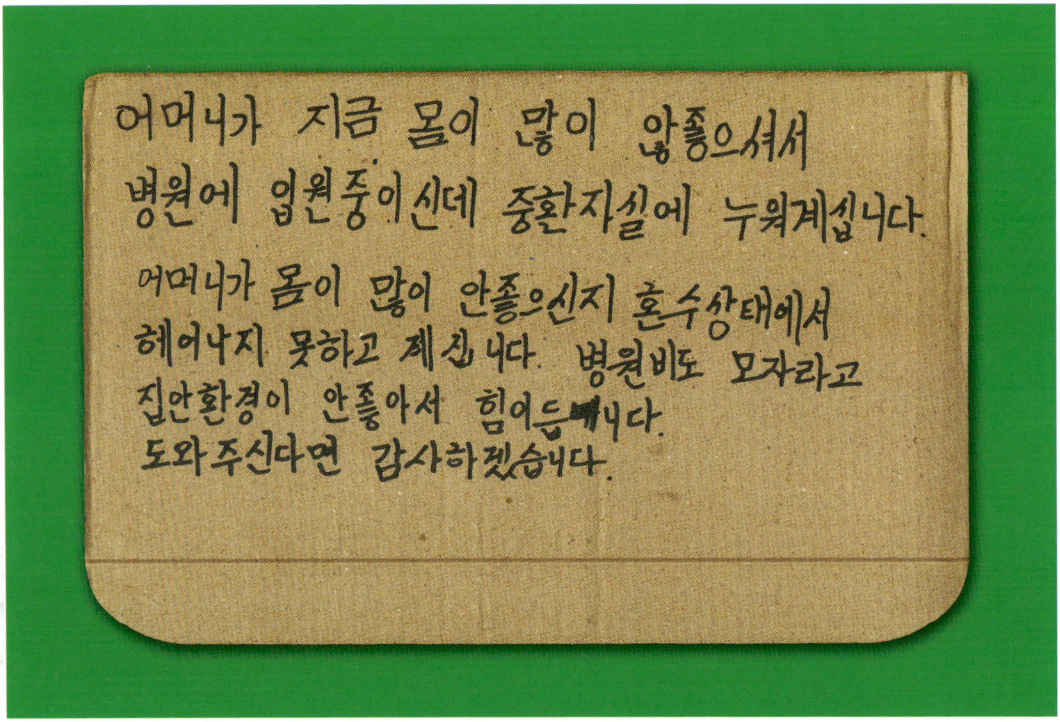
어머니가 지금 몸이 많이 안좋으셔서
병원에 입원중이신데 중환자실에 누워계십니다.
어머니가 몸이 많이 안좋으신지 혼수상태에서
헤어나지 못하고 계십니다. 병원비도 모자라고
집안환경이 안좋아서 힘이듭니다.
도와주신다면 감사하겠습니다.

VILLA CLEMENTINE

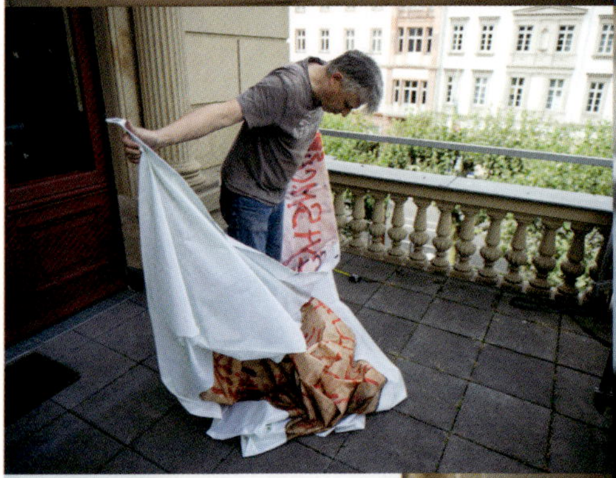

BEACH

PLEASE A

BEACH

SoRRY
Job

Estimado público,
vim por este meio pedir
colaboração, por Deus,
ajude-me, porque faço
Hemodialise 3 vezes por sema-
na e perco muito muito
sangue, ganho pouco e mal
BITTE ICH-HABE
HUNGER
GOTTES-SEGEN
LITERATURHAUS
CAFÉ
Di–So 10–18.30 Uhr
HABE 2 KINDER ZU VERSORGEN
UND HOHE SCHULDEN.
BITTE UM EINE KLEINE
SPENDE. VIELEN DANK!
MERCI S.VP
J'AI FAIM
AIDEZ-MOI
BÜCHER
TAUSCH
STELLE

VILLA CLEMENTINE

PLEASEA

Installation und making off von

FLAGUPY / LITERATUR DER ARMUT ALBRECHT WILD

am Literaturhaus Villa Clementine, Wiesbaden, August 2013

Alle Arbeiten aus der Werkgruppe der »Flaggen« von Albrecht Wild:
verschiedene Maße, Thermosublimationsdruck auf Polyestergewirke, 2009 – 2013

BITTE ICH HABE
HUNGER
GOTTES-SEGEN
LITERATURHAUS
CAFÉ
HABE 2 KINDER ZU VERSORGEN
UND HOHE SCHULDEN.
BITTE UM EINE KLEINE
SPENDE. VIELEN DANK!
MERCI
J.VP
JAI FAH
AIDEZ–MOI
BÜCHER
TAUSCH
STELLE

VILLA CLEMENTINE
PLEASE AFFORD
ME SOME CHANGE
-I MAY BUY A NEW
LITERATURHAUS
CAFÉ

Installation und making off von

FLAGUPY / LITERATUR DER ARMUT ALBRECHT WILD

am Literaturhaus Villa Clementine, Wiesbaden, August 2013

Alle Arbeiten aus der Werkgruppe der »Flaggen« von Albrecht Wild:
verschiedene Maße, Thermosublimationsdruck auf Polyestergewirke, 2009 – 2013

Obdachlos
und Hunger.....
Bitte um eine
Spende Lichen
Dank!
SONO-POVERA
CON-2-BAMBINII
VIPREGO-AIUTATEMI
CON-UNA-PICOLA-
-OFERTA-MANGIARE-
GRAZIE.
OBDACHLOS
Bitte um
Spende Danke

Die folgenden Seiten sind Entwürfe zu der Installation im Mainforum,
IG Metall Hauptsitz, Frankfurt/M.

The following pages are proposal designs for the installation at the Mainforum,
IG Metall Headquarter, Frankfurt/M.

S.V.P. UNE
PIECE
POURMANGER
ZANFA 2EFATES
TICET.RESTAURAT
MERSI.BUCU
Bin in Not, bitte um eine
kleine Spende
DANKE!
MERCI
S.VP
JAI-FAM
AIDEZ-MOI

BITTE ICH-HABE
HUNGER
GOTTES-SEGEN
سبحان الله
بفضل اعاتكم
انني عائش
شكر لكم
POR. FAVOR.AYUDAME
TENGO.3.NINOS.
NOTENGO
TRABAJ.O BUSCO
TRABAJ. ONOTENGO
CASA
MUCIHAS.GRASIAS
SoRRY ANY
Job please help
Me
IHave gotNothiNg
please

Kat.-Nr. 8

Kat.-Nr. 9

te um eine
nde
DANKE!

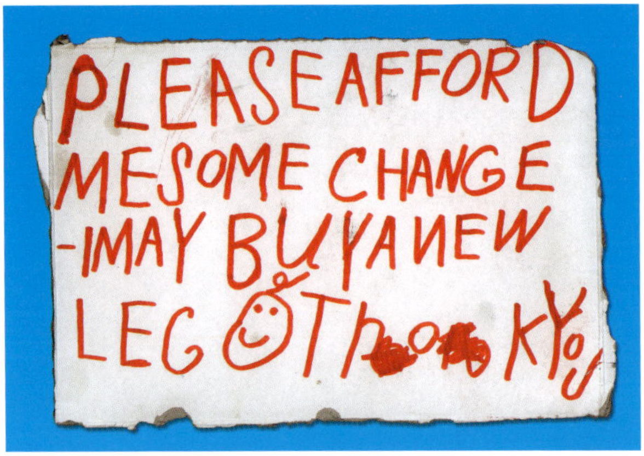
PLEASE AFFORD
ME SOME CHANGE
-I MAY BUY A NEW
LEG Th KYou

ObdachLos
und Hunger.....
Bitte um eine
Spende
Lichen
Dank!

Kat.-Nr. 10, 11

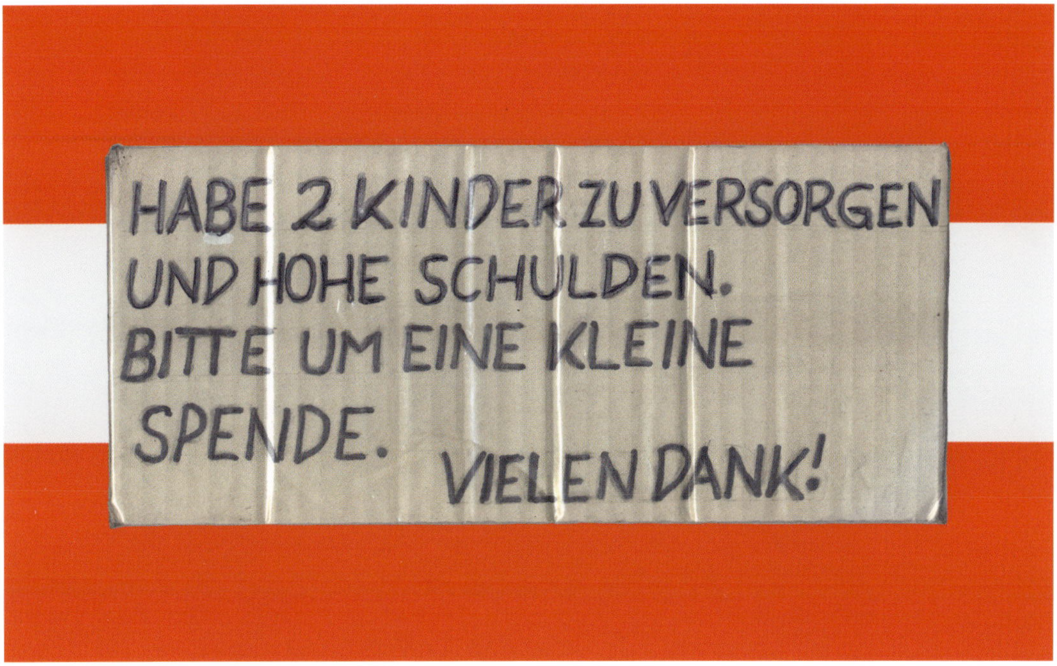
HABE 2 KINDER ZU VERSORGEN
UND HOHE SCHULDEN.
BITTE UM EINE KLEINE
SPENDE.
VIELEN DANK!

Kat.-Nr. 12

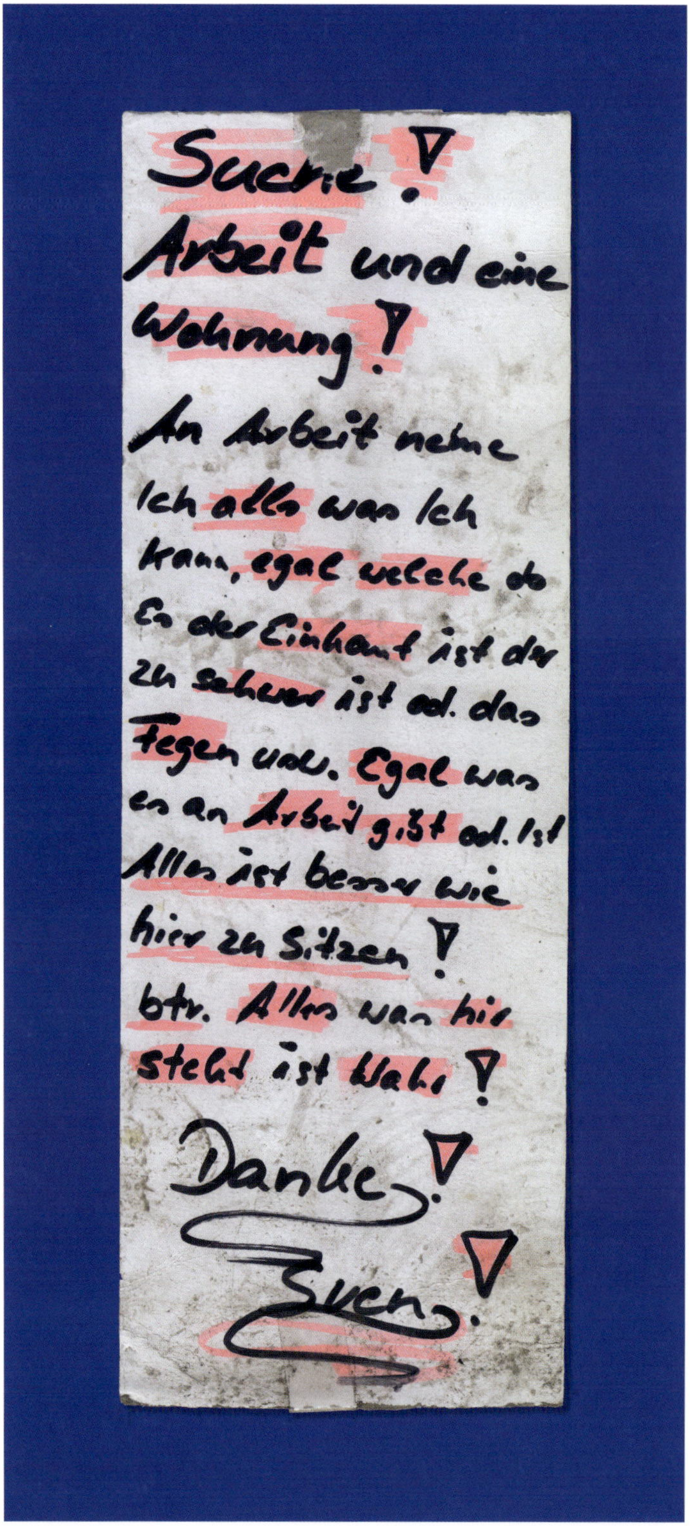
Suche!
Arbeit und eine
Wohnung!
An Arbeit nehme
Ich alles was Ich
kann, egal welche ob
Es der Einkauf ist der
zu schwer ist od. das
Fegen usw. Egal was
es an Arbeit gibt od. Ist
Alles ist besser wie
hier zu Sitzen!
btr. Alles was hir
steht ist Wahr!
Danke!
Sven!

Kat.-Nr. 13

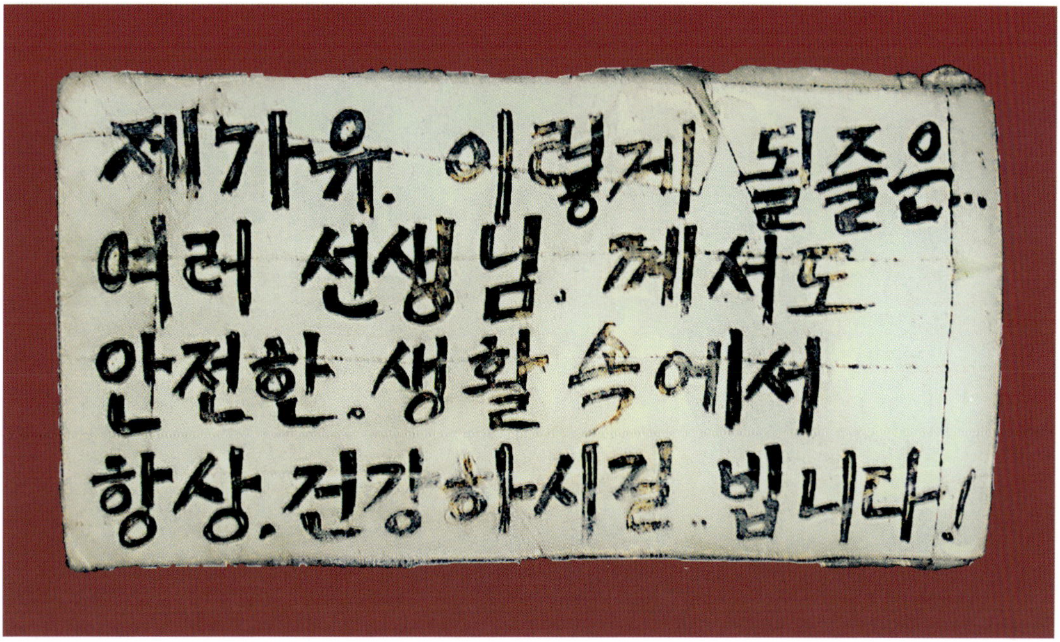
제가유. 이렇게 될줄은...
여러 선생님. 께서도
안전한. 생활 속에서
항상. 건강하시길 빕니다!

제가유. 이렇게 될줄은..
여러 선생님. 께서도
안전한. 생활 속에서
항상. 건강하시길. 빕니다!

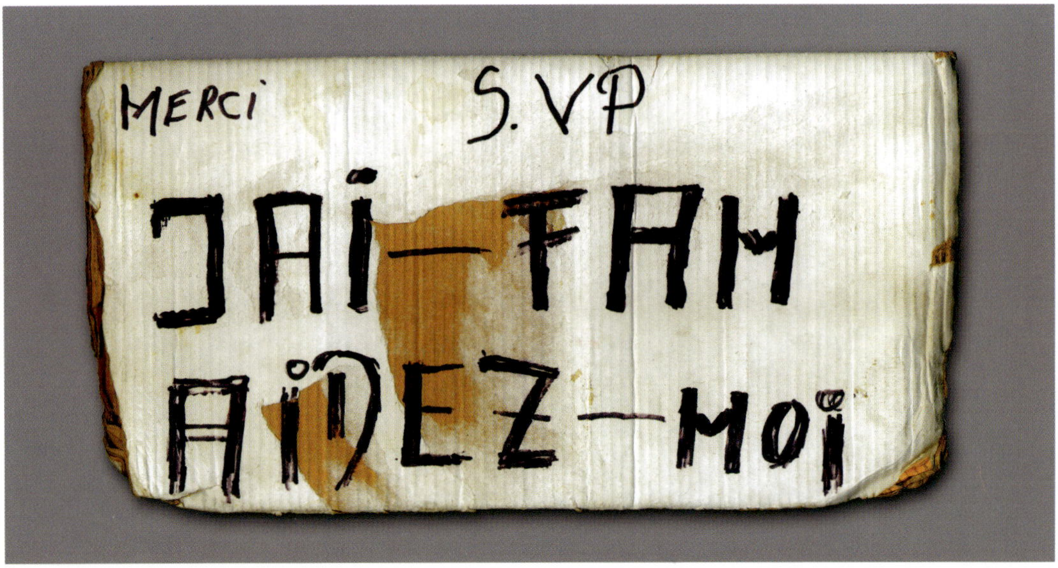
MERCI
S.VP
JAI-FAM
AIDEZ-MOI

Kat.-Nr. 15

VIETNAM
63-71-8YRS-U.S.
HOMELESS VET.
WITH FAMILY+SM.CHILDREN
PLEASE HELP
ANYKIND OF DON.
HAVENT WORKED IN 3 YRS.
THANK

Kat.-Nr. 17

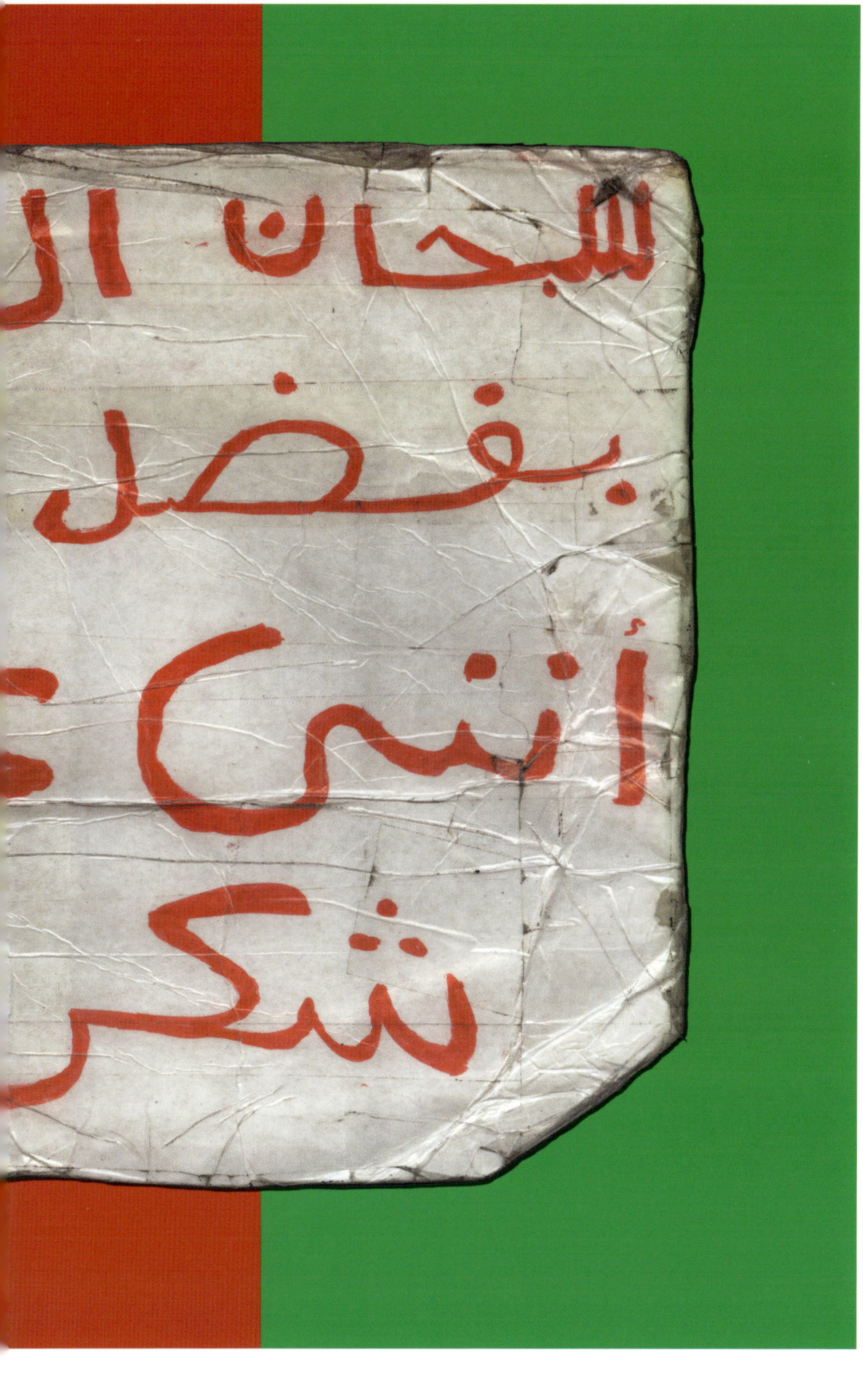
سبحان
بفضل

SONO-POVERA
CON-2-BAMBINIII
VIPREGO-AIUTATEMI
CON-UNA-PICOLA-
-OFERTA-MANGIARE-
GRAZIE.

Kat.-Nr. 18

OBDACHLOS
Bitte um
Spende
Danke

Kat.-Nr. 19

S.V.P. UNE
PiECCE
POVR.MANGER
ZANFA 2EFATES
TiCET.RESTAURAT
MERSi.B:UCU

Kat.-Nr. 20

"That's right, the bank sells, what else should it do?, and the bank buys back, because no one else does it, and the bank buys you, and the bank buys you out and regulates you and regulates you out again."

ELFRIEDE JELINEK, Epilogue to *The Merchant's Contracts: An Economic Comedy,* 21 April 2009[1]

1 From http://www.elfriedejelinek.com/ (accessed on 27 June 2013); English translation by Judith Rosenthal

Flagupy – Literature of Poverty

The neologism "Flagupy" in the exhibition title formulates a form of protest after the manner of the "Occupy Wall Street" movement.[2] It is an act of speech with an imperative character: in addition to "raise the flag", "flag up" can also be interpreted in the sense of "show your colours". Jelinek's drama with the subtitle *An Economic Comedy* is suitable for pointing a way into the topic, because poverty in a society always bears a relation to its wealth. Since the 1990s, poverty has increasingly become a matter not only affecting "the others" outside Europe, but is also once again a topic of greater relevance in Germany.[3] Here we have newly emerging poverty circumstances in which the majority of those affected, while they do not actually suffer hunger, are subjected to many different forms of societal exclusion. Twenty oversize beggars' signs printed on flag cloth against the backgrounds of national flags are on display on the exterior of the Villa Clementine – which houses the Literaturhaus, or House of Literature – in Wiesbaden.[4] Partially concealing the Gründerzeit architecture, the flags make reference to the signs' origins. The artworks thus "impede" the view of the stately facades in a manner of which otherwise only advertising billboards are capable. Wild shows colours:

> **"OBDACHLOS / Bitte um Spende/ Danke** [last word double-underlined]**"** (HOMELESS / Request donation / Thanks)

one of the appeals reads, and the viewer asks himself, justifiably, whether he is supposed to buy something or who could possibly be homeless in the Gründerzeit villa and begging for money. What develops in Albrecht Wild's works is unforeseeable in its effect, and precisely that circumstance is intentional. The artist ar-

---

2 I would like to thank Katharina Menzel-Ahr (Ulm) for the critical discussion of this essay.

3 The much-cited image of the widening gap between the poor and the rich, however, is too simplistic. The imbalance of incomes is increasing in Germany, but that circumstance is not synonymous with increasing poverty. See Kolja Rudzio, "Armut. Steigt der Anteil der Armen in Deutschland? Viele glauben das, und die SPD will im Wahlkampf damit punkten. Doch es stimmt nicht", in *DIE ZEIT*, no. 52, 19 December 2012, p. 24; "Im Gespräch: Klaus Schroeder, Zeithistoriker an der Freien Universität Berlin. 'Armutsforschung ist weitgehend politisch motiviert'", in *Frankfurter Allgemeine Zeitung*, no. 298, 21 December 2012, p. 13.

4 For information on the Literaturhaus in Wiesbaden, see KULTURAMT WIESBADEN (ed.): *Das Literaturhaus Villa Clementine in Wiesbaden* (Regensburg, 2009).

ranges the objects, but they take on a life of their own, they speak of and envision other lives and, as an ensemble, form a multi-vocal work which will be the topic of this essay.

THE RAFT OF THE MEDUSA – THE BEGINNINGS IN LAUSANNE AND SEOUL

Albrecht Wild's critical exploration of the topic of poverty began in 2006 with a contribution to the "Fluid Artcanal International" exhibition project. Carried out in collaboration with the artist Suzanne Wild, the floating installation *Boatpeople* consisted of a raft construction on which clothed shop-window mannequins are raising a white flag (fig. 1). The large plastic bags, the water bottles, the male figure in camo fatigues and one arm in a sling, and the two veiled female figures, one of them lying with a baby mannequin, suggest that the passengers are war – or civil war – refugees. The raft travelled for three months each on the Canal de la Thielle in Switzerland and subsequently on the Gapcheon River in Daejeon (South Korea) – i.e. non-art locations –, where they caused confusion and created a stir.[5] Albrecht Wild also processes that event with photographs in which he mounts the raft. The resulting photomontages show the raft before (for example) the New York skyline as seen from the ferry from Staten Island (fig. 2). The viewers are thus reminded of nineteenth-century immigrants from Europe.[6] New York is a place associated with hopes and longings, and generations of immigrants saw it for the first time from this perspective. At the same time, we might also be reminded of Théodore Géricault's *Raft of Medusa*.[7] The passengers from the shipwrecked "Méduse" came to gruesome fame. According to the reports of two survivors, cannibalism had broken out on the raft, which consisted of wreckage from a vessel sent to Senegal under French flag during the Napoleonic wars of liberation. Géricault's depiction of corpses and other horrors violated the conventions of history painting, and the work caused a scandal when it was exhibited at the Paris Salon in 1819. Originally used to refer to Vietnam War refugees, the term "boat people" which served as the title of Wild's raft is meanwhile associated with waves of migration from all over the world, and above all with the miserable plight of the refugees off the coast of Lampedusa.

Fig. 1: In collaboration with Suzanne Wild, Boatpeople, 2006/07, installation, 240 × 225 × 290 cm, destroyed

A COLLECTION OF BEGGARS' SIGNS

The point of departure for Flagupy is a collection of beggars' signs – meanwhile numbering more than twenty – which the artist documents. For each sign he makes

5 PETER JOCH (ed.), *Albrecht Wild: I didn't expect this to happen to me …*, exh. cat. IASK Changdong National Art Studio Seoul, Korea and National Museum of Contemporary Art Korea (Seoul, 2008), pp. 4–5.

6 Correspondence with the artist on 23 June 2013.

7 THÉODORE GÉRICAULT, *The Raft of the Medusa*, 1818–19, oil on canvas, 491 × 716 cm, Paris, Musée du Louvre. See ALBERT ALHADEFF, *The Raft of the Medusa: Géricault, Art, and Race* (Munich et al., 2002).

Fig. 2: Boatpeople off the Skyline of New York, 2009, photomontage, 225 × 300 cm, property of the artist

a kind of file card based on handwritten notes similar to diary entries and supplemented with a photo.[8] As art material and nucleus, this collection demands an explanation of the role it plays in Albrecht Wild's oeuvre. To begin with, it is important to point out that it is a collection, as opposed to an archive. From the archivist's point of view, notes and memos are worthy of inclusion in archives when they conform to a specific order.[9] Earlier testimonies of poor people have survived because they were preserved in exchange with government authorities and institutions. According to the field of archival science, a collection of written material, on the other hand, is a selected accumulation. Albrecht Wild's collection encompasses objects and recalls persons with whom he had direct contact for the most part. The beggars reacted to his request with surprise; in some cases he had to convince them that, in addition to payment, the compensation would also include the production of a new sign, and in other cases no sale came about. Meanwhile other artists are also involved, in that they agree to bring signs with them from other countries. The travels of Albrecht Wild and the collaborating artists presently mirror the artist's mobility and his network: Frankfurt, Berlin, Paris, Vienna, Budapest, Lisbon, Athens, New York, Cape Town, Seoul, etc. Yet usually owing to circumstances the beggars themselves could not control, they were likewise always mobile as refugees or migrants. The flags sometimes underlying the enlarged signs thus offer no reliable orientation as to the beggars' origins. Statistically, however, poverty is a national economic affair and a political instrument, as is evidenced by the German government's "Armuts- und Reichtumsbericht" (Report on Poverty and Wealth) or unjustified nationalist resentments towards refugees.

Fig. 3: View of the exhibition "Pauvre Luxembourg", 2011, at the Musée d'Histoire de la Ville de Luxembourg

The collection of beggars' signs, which is kept in a large suitcase, also travels. The suitcase serves as a vehicle when, for example, the artist acts as courier and brings works to a museum for an exhibition. If once they were tools of the beggars' trade, when they are shown in a museum, a church or in the studio, the signs can represent various things: souvenirs, objects, loans or autographs. Even if only the original signs are displayed, as in the exhibition *Pauvre Luxembourg* taking place in that country in 2011, the respective context is of decisive significance (fig. 3).[10] The exhibition space in Luxembourg and the form of the display cases – reminiscent of those used for jewellery – "ennobled" the signs

8 This essay is based on the twenty beggars' signs printed on banners for the Wiesbaden exhibition.

9 Mario Wimmer's brilliant study of the emergence of the self-conception of archival science as an archaeology of the language of the archive in the nineteenth century emphasizes the clear distinction between archive and collection from the archivist's point of view. See MARIO WIMMER, *Archivkörper. Eine Geschichte historischer Einbildungskraft* (Constance, 2012), p. 51.

10 MARIE-PAULE JUNGBLUT and CLAUDE WEY (eds.), *Armes Luxemburg? Pauvre Luxembourg?*, exh. cat. Musée d'Histoire de la Ville de Luxembourg (Munich, 2011), pp. 310–13.

and served as an example of the fact that the much-discussed presentation of a collection in a gallery space, the so-called White Cube, by no means leads to the objects' neutralization. The beggars' signs retained their appellative character, but took on new connotations through the presentation form.

BEGGARS' SIGNS AS A LITERATURE OF POVERTY

Beggars' signs can be regarded as a form of functional literature which adheres to certain conventions.[11] From the historians' point of view, they are "testimonies to poverty" and ego documents which have received notice in the past years because they represent individual cases of poverty.[12] Whereas institutions and bureaucracies of poverty relief are well documented, the personal testimonials of poor people in the form of political campaigns have only begun to spark interest more recently, for example when the European Anti-Poverty Network's (EAPN) Voices of Poverty directed attention to the individual poor person who stands out from the collective mass.[13] Against this background, Albrecht Wild's works can also be considered a collection of voices, as it were. In globalized circumstances with migrating artworks, travelling artists and wandering poor people, these works interact worldwide – though it is an interaction sought primarily by artists and curators. At the same time, however, the texts also differ from one another, and in many countries poverty exists, but no beggars' signs. In Japan, for example, a beggar's sign would be inconceivable as a means of asking for alms.[14] In the following I will refer to the texts as a collection of voices, since many of them correspond to the style of spoken language, a characteristic that also applies to older ego documents, for which reason the historian Thomas Sokoll recommends reading petitions and letters aloud.[15]

Fig. 4: Beggars' sign, New York City, corrugated cardboard, acquired in New York in 2009, property of the artist

11 On the subject of economy, labour and literature, see, among others, ELKE BRÜNS (ed.), *Ökonomien der Arbeit. Soziale Verhältnisse in der Literatur* (Munich, 2008); FRANZISKA SCHÖSSLER (ed.), "Arm und Reich in der Literatur", in *Der Deutschunterricht. Beiträge zu seiner Praxis und wissenschaftlichen Grundlegung*, vol. 64/2012, no. 5; NICOLE COLIN and FRANZISKA SCHÖSSLER (eds.), *Das nennen Sie Arbeit? Der Produktivitätsdiskurs und seine Ausschlüsse* (Heidelberg, 2013).

12 The petitionary letters written by poor people in England, for example, have already undergone investigation. See THOMAS SOKOLL, "Selbstverständliche Armut: Armenbriefe in England, 1750–1850", in WINFRIED SCHULZE (ed.), *Selbstzeugnisse der Neuzeit*, vol. 2: *Ego-Dokumente. Annäherungen an den Menschen in der Geschichte* (Berlin, 1996), pp. 227–71. On the German-speaking region, see, among others, AGNES SCZESNY, *Der lange Weg in die Fuggerei – Augsburger Armenbriefe des 19. Jahrhunderts* (Augsburg, 2012); PETER HINTZEN, *"Da ich mir selbst nicht helfen kann". Arme und Armenfürsorge in der zweiten Hälfte des 19. Jahrhunderts, dargestellt im Spiegel der Armenbriefe der Bürgermeister Deutz 1846–1888*, Ph.D. diss. (Universität Trier, 2013).

13 See http://www.eapn.eu/en/news-and-publications/publications/eapn-books/eapn-book-voices-from-the-poverty-line-jobs-and-unemployment-in-the-eu (accessed on 25 June 2013).

14 Conversation with Albrecht Wild on 18 May 2013.

15 THOMAS SOKOLL, "Writing Relief: Rhetoric in English Pauper Letters, 1800–1834", in ANDREAS GESTRICH et al. (eds.), *Being Poor in Modern Europe: Historical Perspectives 1800–1940* (Bern, 2006), pp. 91–111, here p. 109.

It was Vietnam veteran Walt's sign that gave Wild the idea of combining the beggars' signs with national flags, since Walt had decorated his sign with the American flag. The artist Sook Jin-Jo acquired it for Wild in New York in 2009 (fig. 4):

> **"VIETNAM 63–71 8 YRS US.M.C.** [US Marine Corps] **/ HOME-LESS VET. / WITH FAMILY + SM. CHILDREN / PLEASE HELP / ANY KIND OF DON. / HAVENT WORKED IN 3 YRS.** [in the lower right-hand corner:] **THANK YOU WALT"**

In words which have been abbreviated to save space, we learn that Walt served in the Vietnam War as a marine from 1963 to 1971, and that he has a family with small children. Not having had regular employment for three years, he welcomes any kind of contribution. Further information has been added in the upper right and left-hand corners but is rather difficult to decipher from a distance. At the top right: "67-US / KHE SAHN". In other words, in 1967 Walt was in the Vietnamese city of Khe Sanh, where the Marines' Khe Sanh Combat Base was located.[16] In any case, the following words are clearly legible from a distance: "homeless vet.", "with family", "please help" and "any kind of don.". The flag attached to the sign supports the patriotic appeal to the benevolence of the people passing by. When the sign is hung on the outside of the Villa Clementine as a banner, it undergoes a re-contextualization which gives it an added level of meaning; it is now accompanied by a commentary, as it were. Walt's voice is elevated, and the unequal relationship between the benefactor and the recipient is reversed. The potential giver looks up at the building's frieze zone and is confronted with the sign's message from above, i.e. from what is usually the giver's perspective. In a previous exhibition, Wild's approach was characterized as "out of the corner of your eye – right in your face".[17]

Fig. 5: Beggar on Insadong Street in Seoul (South Korea), 2009, photograph, property of the artist

NEW FORMS OF BEGGING

Beggars' signs are functional literature with an appellative function, usually written on corrugated cardboard. The materiality – including the signs of wear and tear – is significant.[18] In a manner similar to a poster asking for donations, the object is to catch the passer-by's attention. At the same time, however, a certain lack of professionality has to be maintained so as not to arouse the suspicion of not being a needy recipient. How professional can a sign look and still be credible? And in which

16 More detailed information on the periods of army service is found in the upper left corner: "I Tour /WBI / 6 NOV- / 2 MAR. / 33R[?] / Trops / NAM[?]N"; upper right: "67– US / KHE / SAHN / 3 RBMBR / 5 BRTT".

17 KUNSTKULTURKIRCHE ALLERHEILIGEN and ANDREAS WÖRSDÖRFER (eds.), *Albrecht Wild: „... aus dem Augenwinkel – RIGHT IN YOUR FACE"*, exh. cat. KunstKulturKirche Allerheiligen and Forum für Moderne Kunst und Neue Musik (Frankfurt/M., 2010).

18 A number of the beggars' signs bear traces of their former owners in the form of fingerprints or hair.

cases is direct contact between the giver and the recipient of the offering still necessary? Why aren't calling cards with beggars' signs on them or LED displays featuring translations of the signs into several languages not acceptable in Europe? These were questions Wild asked himself during his stay in Seoul in 2007/08, a city where rich and poor encounter one another with unmitigated harshness (fig. 5). The numerous photos he took in South Korea also testify to the indifference of the passers-by, who are familiar with these forms of poverty and misery. A lame beggar winds his way along the Insadong, a street in Seoul, on a board on wheels. He also pushes a padded box, likewise on wheels, along in front of him; on top of it is a bowl for alms. The gloves, head covering and stockings, all white, are conspicuous; unlike the passing pedestrians; the beggar hardly shows any skin. Like the signs, these photographs depicting the poignant contrasts between poor and rich in the South Korean metropolis also form a collection in Albrecht Wild's oeuvre. To an extent, this collection is documentary in nature and, as a memory aid, can inspire further works. Yet the photographs can also stand on their own.

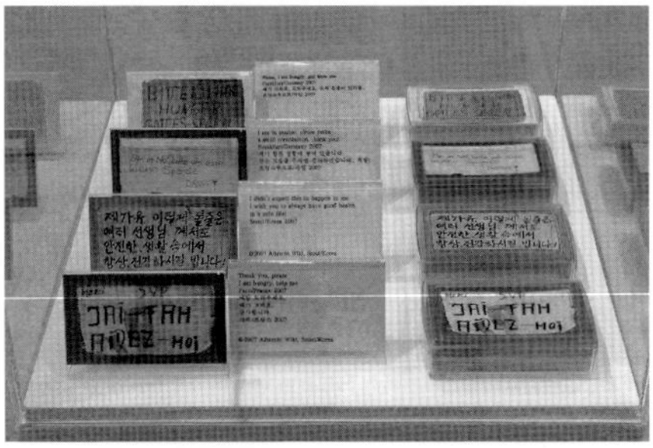

To the question of how professional a beggar's sign is allowed to be, Albrecht Wild responds artistically. All over today's cities, the banners and flickering displays used in advertising vie loudly for our attention; in contrast, the method of begging with handwritten signs seems obsolete. Albrecht Wild's art projects on forms of begging violate boundaries when he enters the handwritten signs in the battle for attention waged by printed and digitalized advertisements. It is this approach that led to Wild's calling cards with printed beggars' signs, pin-back buttons in candy colours, and advertising billboards printed with beggars' signs and incorporated into the Seoul cityscape (figs. 6, 7). His aim with these projects is to take the professionalization of begging to its next logical stage without explicitly addressing the inherent contradictions of doing so. This discussion is left to the viewer – a distribution of roles reminiscent of the socio-critical art of the 1960s and '70s. One example is the digitalization of the beggar's sign in the form of an LED device that can be worn around the neck (fig. 8). With this work, Wild combines technology and begging as a means of interacting with the urban space. The LED ticker technology permits the display of constantly changing texts and adaptation to the respective environment through the entry of the texts in different languages.

Fig. 6: Business Cards, 2007

Fig. 7: Near City Hall, Seoul, 2007, Fictive Advertising Campaign, photomontage

Other artists have developed begging automats as a new art form of begging. Such begging automats have been produced as a response to prohibitions on begging designed to eliminate beggars from the urban setting. A representative example is the begging machine created by Kaspar J. König following a ban on begging in pedestrian zones in Slovenia.[19] The replacement of the human being has an unsettling quality about it. The ban on begging in Styria in 2011, for example, prompted the curators Michael Behr and Astrid Kury to organize the ex-

19 See JUNGBLUT and WEY 2011 (see note 10), pp. 308–09; also see the short film on the object: http://www.youtube.com/watch?v=fgz4Zmx4nkk (accessed on 20 June 2013).

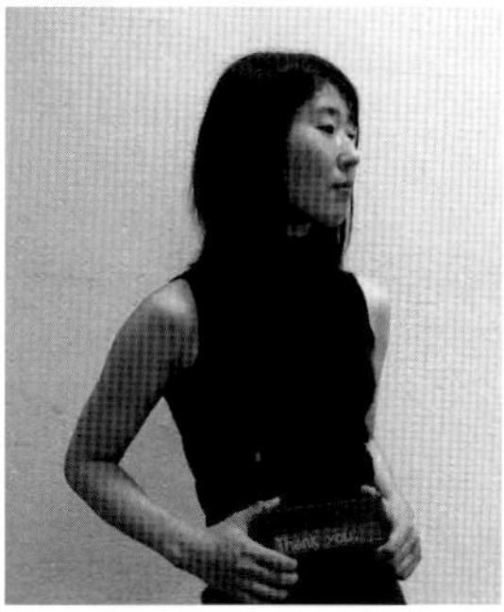

Fig. 8: LED Display for Wearing around the Neck, worn by the artist Zero Reiko Ishihara, 2009

hibition "Wir sind Bettler" (We are beggars), featuring artistic arguments against the politically desired disappearance of beggars from the streets of Graz.[20] A begging automat of the year 2008 by zweintopf on view in the show, for instance, puts a distance between the viewer and the beggar by having the latter present only virtually, by way of a television screen mounted on a shopping cart.

Wild's art bears an affinity to these artistic actions which intervene in socio-political debates. His aim is not to replace the human being with automats, however, but to employ digitalization as an up-to-date begging aid. Within this context, the adaptation to the changed conditions of begging and the introduction of an artistic aesthetic are not mutually exclusive.[21]

TEXT AND IMAGE

The beggars' signs printed on polyester flag cloth and on display in Wiesbaden could be referred to as "text images",[22] since each of the handwritten messages is characterized by a kind of inherent double dynamic. Apart from the presence of the body of writing – for example its graphic design – there is also the representational function of the sign, in that the process of seeing and immediately reading the writing in turn evokes images.[23] Let us consider such texts first as literature and then, in a second step, as images.

The majority of the texts have been composed in simple language. A number of them consist entirely of incomplete sentences: "Bin in Not, bitte um eine / kleine Spende / Danke!" (Am in trouble, request a / small donation /Thanks!; cat. no. 9). Many of the signs from countries in Europe contain references to Christian charity:

"BITTE ICH-HABE / HUNGER / GOTTES-SEGEN"
(PLEASE I-AM / HUNGRY / GOD'S-BLESSING)

holds out the prospect of God's reward and thus follows the tradition of Christian charity and works of mercy, even if benevolence is also an element of other religions, for example zakat in Islam or tzedakah in Judaism.[24] The voice of a beggar's

---

20 See the cooperative exhibition presented by the Akademie Graz and the Stadtmuseum Graz at the Stadtmuseum Graz from 14 April – 4 June 2011. I would like to thank Astrid Kury for sending me the unpublished documentation of the exhibition.

21 On this subject, see *Instant Housing* by WINFRIED BAUMANN, vehicle for homeless persons which can also be purchased by relief organizations. See HERBERT UERLINGS et al. (eds.), *Armut – Perspektiven in Kunst und Gesellschaft*, exh. cat. Stadtmuseum Simeonstift et al. (Darmstadt, 2011), p. 399, cat. no. 151 (Nina Trauth).

22 On the design, see the deliberations by SUSANNE STRÄTLING and GEORG WITTE, "Einleitung", in idem (eds.), *Die Sichtbarkeit der Schrift zwischen Evidenz, Phänomenalität und Ikonizität* (Munich, 2006), pp. 7–20.

23 Ibid., p. 9.

24 See the entries "Zakat" by TONIA SCHÜLLER and "Zedakah" and "Gemilut Chassadim" by RAINER JOSEF BARZEN; idem, "Jüdische Armenfürsorge. 'Ich, der Herr, schaffe Gnade, Recht und Gerechtigkeit'"; SARAH VANESSA LOSEGO, "Sozialfürsorge für französische Muslime 1945–1965", in UERLINGS et al. 2011 (see note 21), pp. 66–67, 82–91, and 311–17.

sign from Seoul says: "I didn't expect this to happen to me. I wish you to always have good health in a safe life." Both texts end with a rhetorical wish formula for the potential giver in a manner reminiscent of European pauper literature of the nineteenth century. The 1824 petition by Ann Marsh, for example, ends with the words: "She [Ann Marsh] will ever acknowledge with grateful thanks to her kind benefactors."[25]

A look at the vocabulary reveals recurring topoi, regardless of nationality: hunger, illness, and unemployment along with the resulting homelessness. Debt and an abundance of children are also cited as reasons for the state of privation. At the same time, the voices differ distinctly in style. Some address the giver with an opening of the kind customary for a speech: "Very honoured public"[26] or, like Sven did, a want ad: "Wanted!".[27] Only very few disclose their names. The contribution being requested also differs. As a rule it is no more than just a small donation – a bit of change or a food stamp – that is requested of us.

> **"Merci S. VP / JAI-FAM** [sic] **/ AIDEZ-MOI"**
> (Thank you PLEASE / I'M HUNGRY / HELP ME).[28]

By starting with a thank-you, however, the usual sequence of a letter, for instance – salutation, body and closing –, is violated. This example shows that the text does not necessarily have to follow the customary direction of reading. It moreover functions situationally: the manner in which "Thank you" and "Please" is reinforced with eye contact is decisive for whether a donation is actually made. The language can also be used in such a way as to address a certain category of persons. For example, English is used to address tourists, while languages such as Arabic are directed towards the beggar's compatriots (cat. no. 17). The voices also have a gender: women cite an abundance of children as the reason for their poverty.

On the whole, the signs use conventional topoi to reveal the beggar's biography for the sake of the alms. The sign is an act of self-disclosure the beggar is compelled to carry out in public. As also witnessed in various shows on commercial television, self-disclosure cuts both ways. In the case of the beggar it does not automatically elicit recognition because it is reduced to his/her poverty or unemployment. In Albrecht Wild's work, the anonymity of the authors is maintained. We read their texts and thus take an interest in their fates without knowing their portraits – unusual in a world which is perceived visually, above all by way of images, to an increasing degree.

25 The petition was probably written by Charles Loosey of Long Alley to the church wardens and committee of the parish of Chelmsford, Essex on behalf of Ann Marsh. See SOKOLL 2006 (see note 15), pp. 97–99.

26 Beggar's sign, Lisbon, 2011, cat. no. 4.

27 Beggar's sign, Frankfurt/M., 2013, cat. no. 13.

28 Beggar's sign, Paris, 2007, cat. no. 15.

TEXT AS IMAGE

A text analysis of beggars' signs would not be complete if it failed to take their design into consideration. The afore-cited sign "MERCI S. VP / JAI-FAM [sic] / AIDEZ-MOI" owes its impact in part to its design: The "THANK YOU" and the abbreviated "PLEASE" appear in smaller letters, probably having been added later to reinforce the appeal for help. The manner in which the space is used is also decisive. We rarely encounter a well-developed handwriting style, since the majuscules most of the authors prefer usually interrupt the flow of the script. Designed to have an impact even from a distance, the letters are usually drawn with wide, dark-coloured markers. The contours of the capitals are generally filled in. The horizontality of the lines is either strictly adhered to, bringing about the impression of a printed text, or departed from with undulations.[29] The space is rarely used freely, as in the sign from Cape Town (cat. no. 6). The form of the sign made of torn cardboard with notches on either side for the hands dictates the position of the text, which is diagonal in part; it consists of majuscules filled in with hatching. On the whole, the handwritten beggars' signs take commercial art and printed advertising as the orientation for their graphic design. In rare cases, coloured illustrations are cut out and glued to the cardboard signs (cat. no. 3). This image of a saint depicts two kneeling women at the left and a shepherd with sheep at the right. The believers gaze up towards an elevated figure of which only the shoes and part of the white robes are visible – the rest of the picture is missing. To judge from the iconography, it could be an Adoration of the Virgin or of Christ.[30] The use of the image of a saint creates a devotional situation, while also reinforcing the message that the woman is sick and has five children. The voice says:

> **"Ich kann nicht arbeiten. Wir danken Ihnen für eine Cabe!** [sic]. (I can't work. We thank you for a donation!)

The kneeling figures in the picture of a saint thus become the recipients of the donation; the readers are animated to perform an act of Christian charity. The image of a saint is also reminiscent of the devotional objects and offerings of thanks from healed persons at pilgrimage sites.

Thus in general, the beggars' signs can also be said to be vehicles of imagery in that the authors arrange the text graphically within the rectangular space, sign them, and/or integrate printed pictures in the overall presentation.

OF CARTELLE AND SIGNS

If we pursue the question as to how long beggars' signs have existed and how the exchange between the benefactor and the recipient has been put into writing, we set out on a journey through the history of the literature of poverty which can merely be touched on in this context. That history is inseparably tied to the history of education and literacy. Many poor people in the past as well as the present were and are unable to read and write. What is more, to this day, the testimonies to the

29 Beggar's sign, Frankfurt/M., flea market, 2007, cat. no. 10.

30 Theoretically, it could also have been an Ascension of Christ, although an Ascension in which Christ is depicted with footwear would be iconographically unusual.

existence of the givers are far greater in number because they were and are considered worthy of being collected.

In the drama literature of ancient Greece, the beggar was an object of mockery and amusement.[31] A graffito which reads "Abomino paupero[s]" (I abominate poor people)[32] is clearly contemptuous. Against the background of antiquity, the religious concept of charity was revolutionary. Before that, there was no religiously formulated need to provide help to the poor in Europe. Many medieval depictions of beggars and the early modern period were executed from the point of view of the Church or of the town that commissioned the work as a means of calling attention to the relief it offered to the poor.[33] In all such depictions, the painted relationship between the donor and recipient of the gift is interesting.[34] Tattered and patched clothing, various forms of physical handicap, the begging bowl or open hand, as well as the beggar's staff and spoon are the attributes of the early modern beggar in painting and printmaking.[35] Here Pieter Brueghel the Younger's *Seven Works of Mercy*, for example, come to mind.[36] Today poor people are occasionally stylized with beggars' signs or bowls because, without such attributes, poverty is no longer clearly recognizable in Western industrial societies. Jogging suits and gym shoes, for instance, have meanwhile become world fashion and are no distinct sign of poverty.

In a number of paintings of the early modern era, texts play an important role. One of the most famous cases in point is Jusepe de Ribera's *Boy with the Club Foot* (1642), who has attached a slip of paper to his crutch bearing the inscription "Da mihi elimo / sinam propter amorem Die" (Give me alms for the love of God).[37] Yet it was presumably not the boy who wrote it, since he probably could not write. Small writing tablets, referred to as "cartelle" in Italian, served in paintings as a means of communication between the viewer, the painter and the patron – but excluded poor people. The exchanges revolve around the right confession and the politics of poor relief as a responsibility of the Church and the State. Beggars required permission

31 PETER KRUMBACH, "Schauspieler und Darsteller in der antiken Gesellschaft", in STEPHAN SEILER (ed.), *Armut in der Antike. Perspektiven in Kunst und Gesellschaft*, exh. cat. Rheinisches Landesmuseum (Trier, 2011), pp. 53–56, here p. 55.

32 Quoted in ibid., p. 8.

33 Whereas early modern depictions of beggars in the fresco programmes of hospitals and churches bear positive connotations, works of printmaking and literature north of the Alps such as the *Liber Vagatorum* stigmatize beggars as crooks. On that subject, see TOM NICHOLS, *Irony and Ideal in Sixteenth-Century Beggar Imagery* (Manchester et al., 2007), p. 6.

34 See PHILINE HELAS, "Repräsentation der Wohltätigkeit. Der Akt des Gebens und Nehmens im Bild zwischen dem 13.–20. Jahrhundert", in LUTZ RAPHAEL and HERBERT UERLINGS (eds.), *Zwischen Ausschluss und Solidarität. Modi der Inklusion/Exklusion von Fremden und Armen in Europa seit der Spätantike* (Frankfurt/M. et al., 2008), pp. 37–63.

35 An early publication on this subject is ELISABETH SUDECK, *Bettlerdarstellungen vom Ende des XV. Jahrhunderts bis zu Rembrandt* (Strasbourg, 1931).

36 PIETER BRUEGHEL THE YOUNGER, *The Seven Works of Mercy*, between 1616 and 1638, oil on wood, 43.3 × 57 cm, Ulm, Museum der Brotkultur. See UERLINGS 2011 (see note 21), p. 359, cat. no. 50.

37 MICHAEL SCHOLZ-HÄNSEL, "Jusepe de Riberas *Der Junge mit dem Klumpfuß* (1642) als Schlüsselwerk der Armenikonographie im Kontext von Konfessionalisierung und Disziplinierung", in ANDREAS GESTRICH and LUTZ RAPHAEL (eds.), *Inklusion/Exklusion. Studien zur Fremdheit und Armut von der Antike bis zur Gegenwart*, 2nd ed. (Frankfurt/M. et al., 2008), pp. 451–78, here p. 461.

Fig. 9: Jani Leinonen: Anything Helps, 2005–09, 22 framed beggars' signs, 53rd Biennale, Danish Pavilion, Venice

to beg, and accordingly carried letters or badges with them as proof of that permission. If the proof was missing or found to be forged, the beggar landed in prison.[38] If we look for the word "Bettelschild" (beggar's sign) in the dictionary by the Brothers Grimm, we will look in vain. What we do find, however, are terms such as "Bettelbrief" (begging letter), "Bettelschelle" (beggar's bell), "Bettelvisite" (beggar's visit), and "Bettelliedlein" (little beggar's song).[39] This word category reveals that the forms of begging in the German-speaking regions were not silent. Beggar-musicians did not require signs. The latter, on the other hand, are seen in documentary photos of the 1930s, when, as a consequence of the Great Depression, people holding signs stood on street corners in search of work.[40] When corrugated cardboard came to be used as packaging for food, corrugated cardboard boxes became objets trouvés used to this day to make beggars' signs and makeshift dwellings.[41] In the twentieth century, the recitation of beggars' appeals fell silent, at least in Europe, when advertising and billboards found their way into cities.[42]

ANYTHING HELPS? – BEGGARS' SIGNS IN CONTEMPORARY ART

Since the 1990s, an increasing number of artists have concerned themselves with matters of the economy, justice, the status of employment in the twenty-first century and its socio-political dimension.[43] The Finnish artist Jani Leinonen's project *Anything helps* differs in fundamental aspects from Albrecht Wild's intention, although Leinonen likewise works with beggars' signs and thinks about modern forms of begging.[44] Let us here consider the beggars' signs exhibited in the Dan-

38 See UERLINGS et al. 2011 (see note 21), p. 377, cat. no. 96 (Nina Trauth).

39 JACOB and WILHELM GRIMM, "Bettelbrief", "Bettelliedlein", "Bettelschelle" and "Bettelvisite", in idem, *Deutsches Wörterbuch,* 16 vols. in 32 fascicles (Leipzig, 1854–1961 and 1971; Quellenverzeichnis), vol. 1, cols. 1727, 1729, 1731, 1733, http://woerterbuchnetz.de/DWB/?sigle=DWB&mode=Vernetzung&lemid=GB05986 (accessed on 12 June 2013).

40 See, for example, a photo of an unemployed stenotypist with a sign, taken in 1930. MATTHIAS REISS, "Zwischen Revolte und Resignation. Das Bild des Arbeitslosen seit dem 19. Jahrhundert", in UERLINGS 2011 (see note 21), pp. 326–35, here p. 333, ill. 220.

41 Corrugated cardboard for packaging merchandise was patented in the U.S. at the end of the nineteenth century; the first European corrugated cardboard factory was founded in 1883. See HEINZ SCHMIDT-BACHEM, *Aus Papier. Eine Kultur- und Wirtschaftsgeschichte der Papier verarbeitenden Industrie in Deutschland* (Berlin, 2011), pp. 680–82. On the subject of cardboard as a material for makeshift dwellings for homeless persons, also see PETRA OELSCHLÄGEL, *Einrichten. Leben im Karton*, exh. cat. Städtische Galerie Villa Zanders (Bergisch-Gladbach, 2008).

42 It remains to be investigated whether there is a causal relationship between the two phenomena or their concurrence is a mere coincidence.

43 See FRANZISKA EISSNER and MICHAEL SCHOLZ-HÄNSEL (eds.), *Armut in der Kunst der Moderne* (Marburg, 2011).

44 See DANIEL BIRNBAUM (ed.), *Making Worlds – Venice, Biennale 53rd International Art Exhibition* (Venice, 2009), vol. 2, pp. 26–31, here p. 30. The work in Venice is not identical to the edition *Anything helps™ 10% of Your Purchase Goes to the Poor (German Edition)* of plastic replicas of original beggars' signs shown in Vilnius, even though at that point in time Jani Leinonen began collecting beggars' signs (correspondence with Jani Leinonen, 27 June 2013). On the work exhibited in 2005, see PAUL SCHMELZER, "New, Improved Beggar Signs" (9 October 2005), in

ish Pavilion of the 2009 Venice Biennale, since the presentation there – as in the previously described Luxembourg example – likewise decisively changed the message conveyed by the art objects (fig. 9).[45] The Danish and Nordic Pavilions were curated by the artists Michael Elmgreen and Ingar Dragset, who interpreted the exhibition spaces as the domiciles of two fictitious private collectors, for which reason the curatorial work was entitled *The Collectors*.[46] Leinonen's work consists of twenty-two beggars' signs with golden frames which decorated the dining room wall in rows of four or five, one above the other. Small brass plaques on the glass bore the names of the cities from which the signs had come. On the artist's homepage, *Anything helps* was declared a monument of guilt and class differences and linked with a donation campaign.[47] Leinonen does not take the position of an admonishing observer, but is part of the overall system: "I want to get rid of class distinction but all I think and do is a result of class distinction."[48] Although the basic material of Albrecht Wild's work is the same as that of Leinonen's, unlike Leinonen Wild does not figure as a person in his project. He does not accompany, document or control the reception of his works with the help of a website as a form of self-presentation. In the tradition of Concept art, the concern of Wild's work is with the search for new forms of artistic expression which offer critique and protest in a different manner.[49] On the other hand, in both cases the contextualization is important for interpreting the works: in Venice the beggars' signs in gold frames were elevated to the status of collectors' items; in the exhibition of Albrecht Wild's works in Luxembourg, the same effect was achieved by way of the display cases. In order to focus more strongly on the signs as examples of the literature of poverty, Wild chose banners in the public realm as the form of presentation for the Wiesbaden show.

FLAG ART – FLAGUPY

The national flags on which the beggars' signs are printed represent a special kind of "frame". They confront the viewers with a mapping of the world by country. The inclusion of the flag as an underlying surface signals a national context; it is a reference to a territory as well as a monument worthy of commemoration in the manner of depictions of national monuments on postcards and the like.[50] As printed objects, the beggars' signs remain recognizable as such; through the passé-partout-like frame, they take on a quality which invites notice. Whereas affirmative as well as

---

http://eyeteeth.blogspot.de/2005/09/new-improved-beggar-signs.html (accessed on 10 June 2013); PERNILLE ALBRETHSEN et al., "Notes on Works and Projects", in LARS BANG LARSEN et al. (eds.), *The Populism Catalogue,* exh. cat. The Contemporary Art Centre, Vilnius et al. (Berlin and New York, 2005), pp. 23–31, here pp. 27–28, ill. p. 106.

45 Leinonen purchased the first beggar's sign, from which the title was taken, in Texas in 2003.

46 PETER WEIBEL and ANDREAS F. BEITIN (eds.), *Elmgreen & Dragset: Celebrity – The One and the Many,* exh. cat. Zentrum für Kunst- und Medientechnologie, Karlsruhe (Cologne, 2011), pp. 207–54, here p. 250.

47 See http://janileinonen.com/en/ (accessed on 5 June 2013).

48 Ibid.

49 Classification by Peter Joch in JOCH, 2008 (see note 5), p. 16.

50 See DANIEL HOHRATH (ed.), *Farben der Geschichte. Fahnen und Flaggen. Aus den Sammlungen des Deutschen Historischen Museums,* exh. cat. Deutsches Historisches Museum (Berlin, 2007).

critical debates on nationalism and patriotism are associated with the flags, the texts are about homelessness, which defies assignment to a flag. What is more, even if it is no problem to print the signs on the flags of the countries in which they were acquired, the flags are no indication of the respective beggars' nationalities.

Patriotic, critical and other uses of national flags look back on a long tradition in art. In the twentieth century, for example, flag and painting became indistinguishable through the excessive processing of the American flag in the oeuvre of Jasper Johns. With patriotic intentions, Claes Oldenburg collaged the American flag with bits of brown corrugated cardboard.[51] In *Mappa*, a series of tapestries, Alighiero Boetti investigated the flag as a means of marking territory and boundary as well as changes of the same. His maps of the world visualize the individual countries in the colours of their respective national flags.[52] By casting the beggars' signs in the national colours, Wild likewise focusses on country, possession and boundary in a manner which is disconcerting – and thus very effective – in combination with the poor people's voices. As already mentioned, this principle of nationality is questionable for the mobile poor people, but also politically meaningful, since that mobility was and is not unbounded. It is controlled by nations with the aid of admission regulations, and the principle of nation and nationality comes to bear in statistical quantifications. Countries enter into competition with one another in the effort to satisfy the United Nations' millennium development aims or to keep poor people out of the home territory by refusing to admit refugees on the strength of the Third-Country or the Dublin Regulation. The disconcertion caused by the national flag in combination with the printed beggar's sign is what constitutes Wild's artistic contribution to the public discussion of poverty. The artist puts his faith in the aesthetic potential of the texts, whose calls for help counter the representative function of the flags. It is a resistive commentary, by all means with "malicious" intentions, according to the artist.

Fig. 10: Simulation with Beggars' Signs at the Stadtmuseum Simeonstift Trier, 2011, photomontage

SIMULATION ART AND REALITY: THE PRESENTATION OF THE BANNERS IN THE PUBLIC RELIGIOUS AND POLITICAL REALM

A simulation carried out at the Stadtmuseum Simeonstift in Trier (fig. 10) can be regarded as groundwork for the project now being carried out in Wiesbaden and Frankfurt. The photomontages serve as aids in simulating, realizing or remembering projects. Within the framework of the preparations for the exhibition "Poverty – Perspectives in Art and Society" staged in Trier in 2011, Wild executed a montage with a photo of the inner courtyard of the Stadtmuseum Simeonstift Trier; the banner project it depicts was not carried to realization. The historical venue of

51 CLAES OLDENBURG, *Big Cardboard Flag*, 1960, 57.2 × 96.5 ×3.8 cm, ink on cardboard collage mounted on panel, private collection (Christie's, New York, 16 November 2006). The flag is intended as a commemoration of the conquest of Provincetown by the first American settlers, where the artist stayed in 1960. See ACHIM HOCHDÖRFER, "Von der 'Street' zum 'Store'. Claes Oldenburgs Pop Expressionismus", in idem (ed.), *Claes Oldenburg: The Sixties,* exh. cat. Museum Ludwig, Köln et al. (Vienna, 2012), pp. 12–71, here p. 38, ill. p. 35.

52 See EVA SCHARRER and ANDREA VILIANI, "Alighiero Boetti", in EVA SCHARRER and KATRIN SAUERLÄNDER (eds.), *Documenta 13. Das Begleitbuch*, vol. 3 (Ostfildern, 2012), p. 46, cat. no. 30.

the Simeonstift, which was founded in 1140, consists of a nearly square building with four wings, and the Porta Nigra, which was used as a collegiate church until its secularization. The act of mounting the beggars' signs in this once-religious setting would have borne a close connection to the Simeonstift's patron saint. Simeon the Greek had himself locked up in the East Tower of the Porta Nigra and lived there as a hermit in voluntary poverty. Soon after his death in 1035 he was canonized, the Roman gate building was converted into a double church over Simeon's grave, and a canonical abbey founded.[53] In the photomontage, not all of the signs are printed on national flags, and the banners do not adhere to the rhythm of the arcades, but form a frieze which – owing to the underlying colours – seem entirely out of place against the historical architecture. A comparison with the simulation of the inner courtyard of the IG-Metall Building provides evidence of how the architecture and the setting contribute to determining the works' impact (fig. 11). Modern architecture lends itself better to association with banner or billboard advertising; it supports the work of the IG Metall (metalworkers' union) and integrates easily in union campaigns in the struggle for fair working conditions and pay. The members of the Vereinte Dienstleistungsgewerkschaft (ver.di; United Services Union) – after the IG Metall the second largest member of the German trade union federation – likewise provocatively exploit pauper literature in their fight against wage dumping. A sign carried by protestors at a recent demonstration in Frankfurt featured the text "Hey Boss, haste mal 'nen ... [Euro?]" (Hey boss, can you spare a ... [Euro?]).[54] In the struggle for higher pay, the practice of begging is performed as a kind of satire.

Fig. 11: Simulation with Beggars' Signs in the Inner Courtyard of the IG Metall Building in Frankfurt/M.

Fig. 12: Seated Figure, 2008, various materials, 70 × 70 × 55 cm, property of the artist

The signs in the Simeonstift collage, on the other hand, are perceived much more strongly as foreign bodies. Ultimately the exhibition presented a seated figure in combination with an LED display showing pauper literature; this work by Albrecht Wild formed the show's conclusion on the second upper floor (fig. 12).[55] This proved to be so unexpectedly contrary to what is customarily expected at a museum exhibition that the visitors reacted to the artwork by adopting the role of the benefactor and giving the figure money. These offerings continued throughout the show.

In 2010, Wild realized a direct juxtaposition between banners and a seated figure in the Allerheiligenkirche (All Saints' Church) of Frankfurt, although there the banners bore a greater resemblance to posters since they hung flush with the wall (fig. 13). The figure on the right side of the nave is not wearing tattered clothing and has no begging bowl – in other words it does not adhere to the common beggar iconography described above; what is more, it hides its face and sits on the church's stone floor. It is only when it is perceived in conjunction with

53 ELISABETH DÜHR et al. (eds.), *Stadtgeschichte im Stadtmuseum. Begleitband zur neuen stadtgeschichtlichen Ausstellung im Stadtmuseum Simeonstift Trier* (Trier, 2007), pp. 35–37.

54 Dc. Berlin, "Handel wehrt sich gegen Vorwurf des Lohndumpings", in *Frankfurter Allgemeine Zeitung*, no. 134, 13 June 2013, press photograph by Bernd Kammerer, p. 11.

55 UERLINGS 2011 (see note 21), p. 400, cat. nos. 153–54 (Nina Trauth).

the literature of poverty in the banners that its meaning becomes clear. More so than the art space, the religious space facilitates the confusion of the artwork with a real person. Churchgoers invited Wild's installation to take a seat in the pews. Like the visitors to the poverty exhibition in Trier, the persons in charge wanted to eliminate this ambiguity by adding a donation bowl, and thus to simplify Wild's installation as unequivocal "poverty art" with appellative character.

THE ART OF CRITIQUE

Let us conclude by recapitulating the various lines of thought pursued in this essay. Albrecht Wild's beggars' signs are a collection of a special kind, with an artist as the collector, curator and witness. Yet these signs are not the artwork itself, but vocal material. For Wild, beggars' signs are a form of pauper literature worthy of collection. He uses beggars' signs and photographs serving as aides de mémoire to make installations consisting of seated and lying figures. The banners featuring the beggars' signs are thus only one aspect of his exploration of forms of begging and the artistic material. Wild's works provide impulses for perceiving the topic of poverty in a new way, and taking new perspectives on it. Yet that is not the extent of his art, which bears an affinity to Concept art. The artist is not primarily concerned with actionism in the sense of a simple, propagandistic *anti*-poverty statement – the kind of statement to which art revolving around the theme of poverty is often reduced. In his work – and not only his – openness and ambiguity run the risk of being demoted to the level of narration.

A characteristic aspect of his approach is the translation into new contexts, so that, with his "social" art at non-art venues the boundary between the work, the viewer and the surroundings become hazy and spark actions in the social realm that become a part of the work. This consequence is indebted to the phenomenon of poverty, but also to the artist's specific personal touch, which only becomes apparent at second sight: Albrecht Wild shapes and initiates the space of society. In the process, he does without a straightforward story of the kind formulated, for example, by popular media formats and appellative anti-poverty art, and puts his trust in the aesthetic potential of the literature of poverty. If the Wiesbaden press were to react to the House of Literature with its banner enhancement with the headline "City in an uproar",[56] we would have Wild's work to thank for it. The disruptive potential achieved with the simplest means is one form of "social" art which, in a manner similar to the Occupy movement, takes its aesthetic and socio-political course parallel to familiar media discourses and visual representations. Art as a nuisance factor is one means of voicing critique. Let critique here be understood in keeping with Michel Foucault as an "art of voluntary inservitude, of reflective indocility".[57] It opposes patronization by the state

Fig. 13: Cowering Figure, 2010, various materials, 60 × 43 × 78 cm, property of the artist (installation in Allerheiligenkirche in Frankfurt/M.)

56 Contribution to the Theater Trier festival "Maximierung Mensch", see www.tufa-trier.de/veranstaltungen/detailansicht/article/Stadt-in-Aufruhr.html (accessed on 15 June 2013).

57 These forms of critique respond to the increasing patronization of individuals brought about by a clustering of practices the French philosopher Michel Foucault referred to as governmentalization. Foucault elucidated the concept as follows: "And if governmentalization

authorities and the media, which counter the topic of begging with a repetitive canon of "politically correct" forms of depiction, or by prohibiting it.

POSTSCRIPT

In 1873, just a few years before the Villa Clementine was built, a "bread riot" erupted in Wiesbaden. The German term used at the time – "Brotkrawall" – is no longer in use today: in Germany food riots are a thing of the past.[58] "Krawall" (pronounced "kra-VAHL"), which came into use in the Vormärz, the period from 1815 to 1848, is an onomatopoeic word for turmoil or uproar.[59] The Wiesbaden bread riot, however, was more than loud protest against supposedly exorbitant bread prices. In the thriving Wiesbaden of the Gründerzeit era, brick makers, journeymen and domestic workers were fighting against state authority and for fair wages.[60] As punishable offenses, protests of that kind were on a par with begging. Hugo von Strauss, for example, the Wiesbaden police commissioner, wrote in 1874: "To date, despite the greatest pursuit efforts, begging has not diminished."[61] The exhibition of Albrecht Wild's works in the twenty-first century commemorates those events, even though it was not the history of the place that sparked the idea for the installation. Unlike the riots of earlier times, now it is a visual form of "Krawall" that arouses attention.

---

is indeed this movement through which individuals are subjugated in the reality of a social practice through mechanisms of power that adhere to a truth, well, then! critique will be the art of voluntary insubordination, that of reflected intractability. Critique would essentially insure the desubjugation of the subject in the context of what we could call, in a word, the politics of truth", quoted from MICHEL FOUCAULT, *"What is Critique?"*, in idem, *The Politics of Truth*, 2nd ed. (Los Angeles, 2007), pp. 41–82, here p. 47.

58 HORST STEFFENS, "Der Wiesbadener Brotkrawall von 1873. Ursachen und Hintergründe sozialer Protestbewegungen in den frühen 1870er Jahren", in *Nassauische Annalen. Jahrbuch des Vereins für nassauische Altertumskunde und Geschichtsforschung 100* (1989), pp. 175–96.

59 "Krawall", in GRIMM 1854–1961 and 1971 (see note 39), vol. 11, cols. 2125–2127, here col. 2125, http://woerterbuchnetz.de/DWB/?sigle=DWB&mode=Vernetzung&lemid=GK13019 (accessed on 12 June 2013).

60 STEFFENS 1989 (see note 58), p. 185.

61 Ibid., p. 190.

ICH BIN KRANK
OPERIERT, HABE 5
KINDER UND SIE HABEN
HUNGER. ICH KANN NICHT
ARBEITEN. WIR DANKEN
IHNEN FÜR EINE GABE!
DANKE.

PLEASE AFFORD
ME SOME CHANGE
- I MAY BUY A NEW
LEGO Thank You

KÉREM SEGITSENEK
EGY GYEREKEM VAN
MAGUK SEGEDELME
NÉLKÜL ÉHEZNÉK!
KÖSZÖNÖM SZÉPE

어머니가 지금 몸이 많이 안좋으셔서
병원에 입원중이신데 중환자실에 누워계십니다.
어머니가 몸이 많이 안좋으신지 혼수상태에서
헤어나지 못하고 계십니다. 병원비도 모자라고
집안환경이 안좋아서 힘이듭니다.
도와주신다면 감사하겠습니다.
HABE 2 KINDER ZU VERSORGEN
UND HOHE SCHULDEN.
BITTE UM EINE KLEINE
SPENDE.
VIELEN DANK!
VIETNAM
HOMELESS VET.
WITH FAMILY
PLEASE HELP
ANY KIND OF DON
THANK
ΕΙΜΑΙ ΑΡΩΣΤΟΣ
ΕΙΜΑΙ ΑΣΤΕΓΟΣ
ΒΟΗΘΗΣΤΕ ΜΕ
ΕΥΧΑΡΙΣΤΩ ΠΟΛΥ!!

제가유. 이렇게 될줄은..
여러 선생님. 께서도
안전한. 생활 속에서
항상. 건강 하시길. 빕니다!
Suche!
Arbeit und eine
Wohnung!
An Arbeit nehme
Ich alles was Ich
kann,
Alles ist besser wie
hier zu Sitzen!
btw. Alles was hier
steht ist Wahr!
Danke!
Sven!
62 Estimado público,
Vim por este meio pedir
a vossa ajuda e a vossa
Colaboração, por Deus,
ajude-me, porque faço
Hemodialise 3 vezes por sema-
na e perco muito muito
Sangue, ganho pouco e mal
Obrigado!

Die vorangehenden Seiten sind Entwürfe zu der Installation im Mainforum, IG Metall Hauptsitz, Frankfurt/M.

The previous pages are proposal designs for the installation at the Mainforum, IG Metall Headquarter, Frankfurt/M.

NOTIZEN

Berlin, 2012

Frankfurt/M., 2008

Lissabon, 2011

Frankfurt/M., 2009 · Paris, 2011

Seoul, 2013

Rom, 2011

Seoul, 2008

Wien, 2012

Barcelona, 2010. Foto: © Florence Isabel Wild

Seoul, 2013

OBJEKTE

Folgende Doppelseite: Boatpeople vor der Kulisse von New York, 2009, Fotomontage, 225 x 300 cm, Digitalprint auf PVC-Folie, Besitz des Künstlers (Ausschnitt)

Boatpeople 2006/07 (mit Suzanne Wild), 240 x 225 x 290 cm, zerstört,
Installation auf dem Canal de la Thielle, Schweiz zu *Fluid Artcanal International*.
© Foto: Christoph Stöh Grünig, Biel, Schweiz

Boatpeople Wolmido/Incheon, Südkorea, Fotomontage 2008

Installation in der IASK Changdong
National Art Studio Gallery, Seoul 2008
(Trolley und Liegender, verschollen)

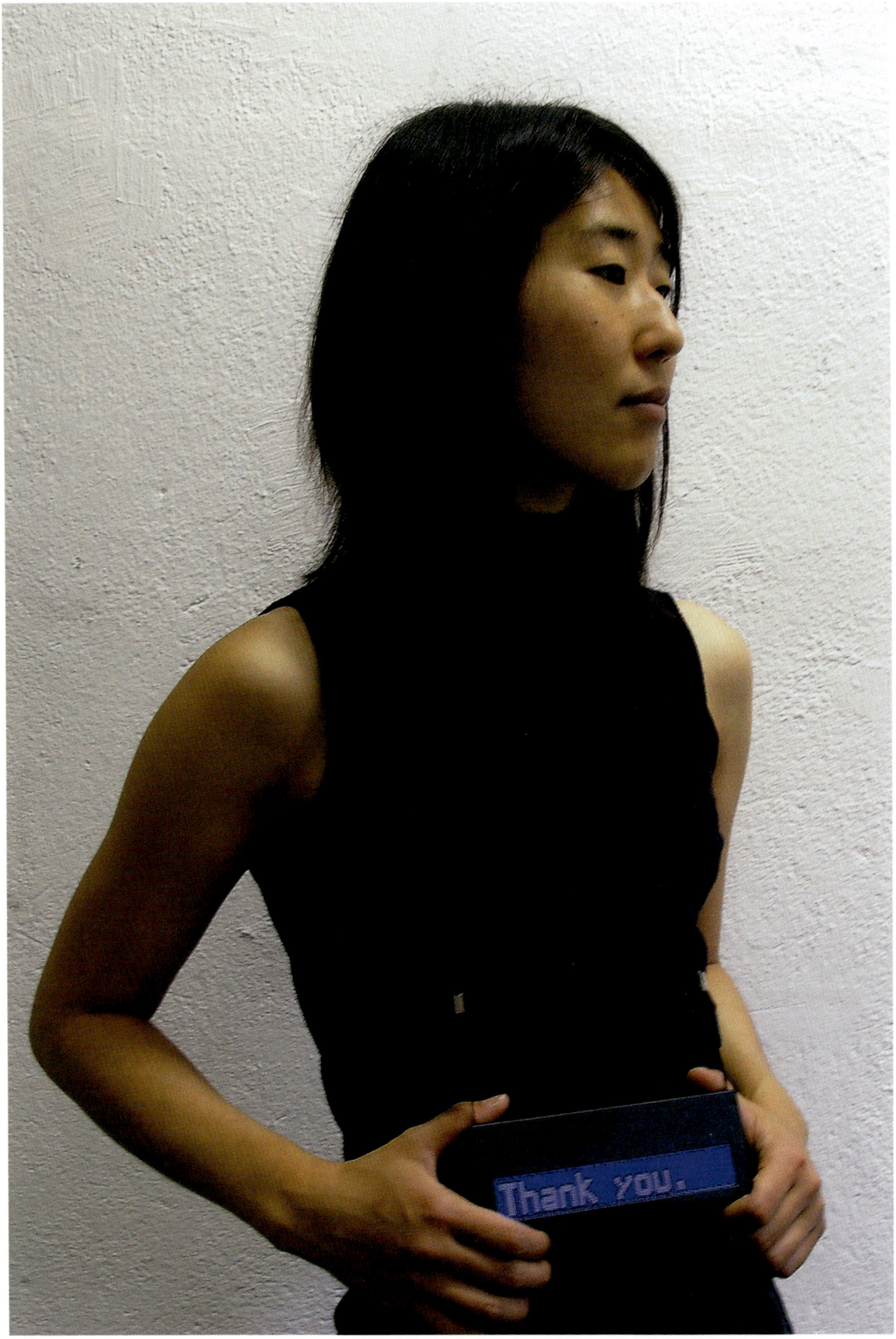
Thank you.

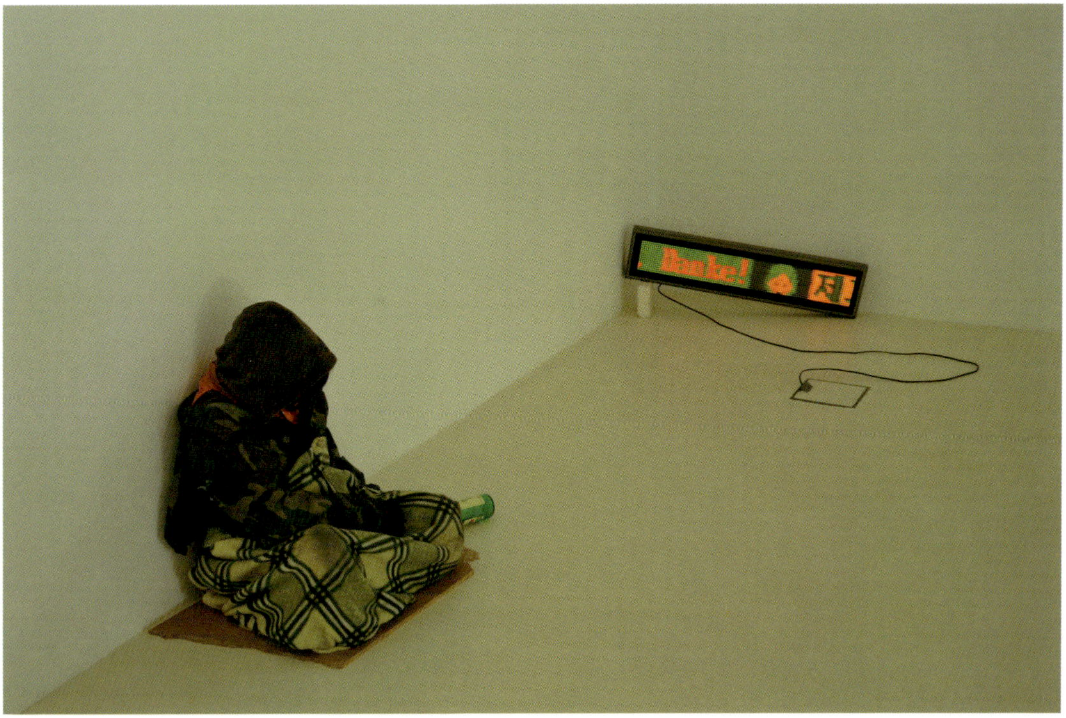

Tragbare Laufschrift, 2009, Edition 1/4, 8 x 16,5 x 1,2 cm, Sammlung Museum Goch / Niederrhein.
Hier getragen von Zero Reiko Ishihara

Sitzender, 2008, 70 x 70 x 55 cm, Besitz des Künstlers, Installation im Stadtmuseum Simeonstift Trier 2011,
zu *Armut – Perspektiven in Kunst und Gesellschaft.* © Foto: Bernhard Matthias Lutz, Trier

HUNGER
GOTTES-SEGE

Installation in der Gallery KunstDoc, Seoul 2009. © Foto: Suzanne Wild

Installation in der Gallery KunstDoc, Seoul 2009. © Foto: Suzanne Wild

Installation in der Gallery KunstDoc, Seoul 2009. © Foto: Cho Young Ha, Wolganmisool Monthly Art Magazine, Seoul

Business Cards, 2007

Buttons, 2007

Werkverzeichnis

Kat.-Nr. 1 — **Bitte helft mir. Ich habe 3 Kinder. Habe keine Arbeit. Suche Arbeit. Bin obdachlos. Vielen Dank** / *Please help me. I have 3 children. Have no work. Looking for work. Am homeless. Thank you very much.*
Schwarzer Filzstift auf brauner Wellpappe, 26,5 x 30,5 cm, Barcelona 2009

Kat.-Nr. 2 — **Ich bin krank – obdachlos – Helfen sie mir – Vielen Dank!!!** / *I am sick – homeless – help me – thank you very much !!!*
Schwarze Farbe auf hellgrauer Wellpappe, 50 x 38 cm, Athen 2013

Kat.-Nr. 3 — **Ich bin krank – operiert, habe 5 Kinder und sie haben Hunger. Ich kann nicht arbeiten. Wir danken Ihnen für eine C**[G]**abe! Danke.** / *I am ill – operated on, have five children and they are hungry. I cannot work, we thank you for a donation ! Thank you.*
Schwarzer Kugelschreiber auf brauner Wellpappe, gefaltet, rechts oben aufgeklebtes ausgeschnittenes farbiges Bildchen (kniende betende Kinder, Schafe vor einer Figur auf einer Wolke schwebend, abgerissen (wahrscheinlich Jesus)), 16 x 27,6 cm (Rückseite weiße Wellpappe mit Aufdruck „6 x 750ml"), vor der Gedächtniskirche am Kurfürstendamm, Berlin 2012

Kat.-Nr. 4 — **62** [Jahre alt] **Sehr geehrtes Publikum, ich möchte auf diesem Wege um Ihre Hilfe und Mitarbeit bitten, bei Gott, helfen Sie mir, weil ich 3 Mal in der Woche zur Hämodialyse muss und zu viel Blut verliere und zu wenig verdiene um Medikamente zu kaufen. Vielen Dank!** / *62* [yrs.] *Dear audience, this way I want to ask for your assistance and cooperation, by God, please help me as I have to go 3 times weekly to the hemodialysis and I am losing too much blood, but I don't earn enough money in order to buy the drugs. Thank you very much!*
Schwarzer Filzstift auf brauner Wellpappe, gefaltet, 27 x 36 cm, Rua Garrett, Lissabon 2011

Kat.-Nr. 5 — **Ich bitte Sie uns zu helfen. Ich habe ein Kind. Ohne Ihre Hilfe verhungern wir! Vielen Dank** / *I ask you to help us. I have a child. Without your help we will starve! Thank you very much*
Schwarzer Marker auf hellgrauem Plastik, 20,7 x 39,5 cm, (Rückseite ebenfalls betextet), Oktogon Metro Station, Budapest 2010

Kat.-Nr. 6 — **Entschuldigung, nehme jede Arbeit an – Bitte helft mir – Ich habe nichts – bitte** / *sorry any job – please help me – I have got nothing – please*
Schwarzer Filzstift auf brauner Wellpappe, gefaltet, 46 x 56 cm, Kapstadt, Südafrika 2011

Kat.-Nr. 7 — **Meine Mutter ist sehr krank, sie ist im Krankenhaus und liegt im Koma und braucht Behandlung, aber ich kann die Operation nicht bezahlen. Ich habe große Probleme. Ich wäre für ihre Hilfe sehr dankbar.** / *My mother is really sick right now, she is in hospital, she is in a coma and needs treatment but I cannot pay for the operation. I am in trouble. If you help me I would appreciate it.*
Schwarzer Filzstift auf brauner Wellpappe, vollständige Pappkiste, 9 x 27,5 x 16 cm, ausgeklappt 9 x 27,5 x 32 cm, Jonggak Underground Station, Seoul 2008

Kat.-Nr. 8 — **Bitte ich-habe Hunger – Gottes Segen** / *Please – I am hungry – God bless you*
Schwarzer Filzstift auf brauner Wellpappe, 26,5 x 36,5 cm, (Rückseite : eingeschweißter Lieferschein, adressiert an: „Interessengemeinschaft Frankfurter Kreditinstitute G.m.b.H."), Konstablerwache, Frankfurt/M. 2007

Kat.-Nr. 9 — **Bin in Not, bitte um eine kleine Spende. Danke!** / *I am in trouble, request a small donation. Thank you!*
Schwarzer Kugelschreiber auf weißer Wellpappe, oberer Rand umgefaltet, orange-rosa bedruckt, 14,5 x 31,5 cm (Rückseite Aufschrift „SWEETDAY"), Zeil, Frankfurt/M. 2007

Kat.-Nr. 10 — **Bitte gebt mir Kleingeld – vielleicht kann ich dann ein neues Bein kaufen ☺ Danke**
Please afford me some change – I may buy a new leg ☺Thank you
Roter Filzstift auf hellgrauem Karton, 24 x 35 cm, Flohmarkt am Museumsufer, Frankfurt/M. 2007

Kat.-Nr. 11 — **Obdachlos und Hunger ... Bitte um eine Spende – ♥lichen Dank !**
Homeless and hungry ... please donate – my (♥) felt thanks!
Schwarzer Filzstift, pinker Textmarker auf weißes Papier, mehrfach gefaltet, 20,6 x 29,4 cm (Rückseite : Speisekarte des japanischen Sushi-Restaurants „Superkato"), Römerberg, Frankfurt/M., 2007

Kat.-Nr. 12 — **Habe 2 Kinder zu versorgen und hohe Schulden. Bitte um eine kleine Spende. Vielen Dank!** / *Have 2 children to take care of and high debts. I request a small donation. Thank you very much!*
Silber-Lackstift, blauer Filzstift, Kugelschreiber und Tipp-ex auf hellgrauer Wellpappe, rundum mit Klarer Folie versiegelt, 24,5 x 10,7 cm (Rückseite farbiger Druck milfina), Rotenturmstrasse nähe Stephansdom, Wien 2012

Kat.-Nr. 13 — **Suche! Arbeit und eine Wohnung! An Arbeit nehme ich alles was ich kann, egal welche, ob Es der Einkauf ist der zu schwer ist od. das Fegen usw. Egal was es an Arbeit gibt od. ist. Alles ist besser wie hier zu sitzen! btr. Alles was hier steht ist wahr! Danke! Sven!**
Wanted! Work and a flat! I take any kind of work, anything that I can do, no matter what, I carry shopping that is much too heavy or sweeping etc. Doesn't matter what kind of work it is, everything is better than sitting here! re. Everything on this sign is true! Thank you! Sven!
Schwarzer Filzstift und pinker Marker auf weißem Karton, oben und unten durchsichtiges Tesaband, Fußabdrücke, 36,7 x 13 cm (Rückseite farbiger Druck BELDAY HOME, 150x200cm, Mikrofaser-Felldecke. flauschig weich, warm und anschmiegsam), Schweizerstrasse nähe Woolworth, Frankfurt/M. 2013

Kat.-Nr. 14 — **Ich hätte nicht gedacht dass mir das passieren könnte ... Ich wünsche Dir ewige Gesundheit in einem guten Leben !** / *I didn't expect this to happen to me ... I wish you to always have good health in a safe life!*
Nur als Fotografie vorhanden! Artsec auf Holz montiert, 22,5 x 22,5 x 3,2 cm, 2008, Dongdaemun Underground Station, Seoul 2007

Kat.-Nr. 15 — **Danke – Bitte – Ich habe Hunger – Helft mir** / *Thank you – Please – I am hungry – Help me*
Schwarzer Filzstift auf weißer Wellpappe, gefaltet, Vorder- und Rückseite beschriftet, 17 x 32 cm, Boulevard des Batignolles, Paris 2007

Kat.-Nr. 16 — **Vietnam 63-71 – 8 Jahre. US.M.C. 67-US / KHE SAHN Obdachloser Veteran mit Familie + Kleinkindern. Bitte um Hilfe. Jede Art von Spenden willkommen. Seit 3 Jahren keine Arbeit. Danke – Walt** / *Vietnam 63-71 8 YRS. US.M.C. 67-US / KHE SAHN Homeless vet. with family + sm. children. Please help. Any kind of don. Haven't worked in 3 yrs. Thank you – Walt*
Roter und schwarzer Filzstift auf braune Wellpappe, mehrfach gefaltet, 32 x 45 cm, Amerikanische Fahne, Stoff, Plastik, 15,5 x 28 cm, New York City 2009

Kat.-Nr. 17 — **Wegen Euch [Eurer Hilfe] kann ich leben!** [wahrscheinlich ein Koran-Zitat] **Vielen Dank /** ***Because of you [your help] I can live!*** [probably quote from the Koran] ***Thank you***
Roter Filzstift auf weißer Pappe, rundum ganzflächig mit durchsichtigem Band beklebt, 33 x 48 cm, Marché Belleville, Boulevard de Belleville, Paris 2012

Kat.-Nr. 18 — **Bin arm – mit 2 Kindern** [quer:] **allein erziehend – Bitte helfen sie mit einer kleinen Spende zum Essen – Danke.** ***/ I am poor – with 2 children*** [at right angle:] ***single parent – Please help with a small donation for food – Thank you.***
Schwarzer Filzstift auf brauner Wellpappe, gefaltet, 24,5 x 30 cm, (Rückseite farbiger Motivdruck „Fragolino" – Rotwein), Via Vittorio Emanuele Orlando, Rom 2011

Kat.-Nr. 19 — **Obdachlos. Bitte um eine Spende. Danke** ***/ Homeless. Request a donation. Thank you***
Blauer Kugelschreiber auf brauner Wellpappe, 24 x 33 cm, Zeil, Frankfurt/M. 2007

Kat.-Nr. 20 — **Bitte ein** [Geld-] **Stück zum Essen – Habe 2 Kinder.** [Nehme] **Essensmarke – Vielen Dank** / ***Please a coin for food. – I have 2 children.*** [will take] ***meal voucher. – Thank you very much***
Blauer Filzstift auf brauner Wellpappe, gefaltet, 26,5 x 29,5 cm, Avenue de la Liberté, Luxembourg 2011

Biografie

***1959** in Weinheim/Bergstr.; **1984 –1990** Studium an der Staatlichen Hochschule für bildende Künste „Städelschule“ Frankfurt/M. **1984 –1990**, Meisterschüler bei Thomas Bayrle sowie **1986/87** an der Slade School of Fine Art, University College London bei Bruce McLean; lebt und arbeitet in Frankfurt/M.

2007/08 Artist-in-Residence (IASK Changdong Art Studio), The National Museum of Contemporary Art, Seoul, **2006** Gastatelier der Stadt Neuchâtel; **1991** Jahreskunstpreis der Frankfurter Künstlerhilfe e.V., Frankfurt/M.; **1989** Jahresstipendium des Lions Club International, Frankfurt/M.; **1988** Erasmus-Stipendium für Großbritannien

Einzelausstellungen (Auswahl): 2012 Galerie Alexandra Erlhoff, Berlin; **2011** Ausstellungshalle 1A, Frankfurt/M. (mit Andreas Exner und Ulrich Becker); **2010** KunstKulturKirche Allerheiligen Frankfurt/M.; **2009** Gallery KunstDoc, Seoul; **2008** The National Art Studio Gallery, Changdong, Seoul; **2005** IHK Frankfurt/M., in Zusammenarbeit mit Städel Museum; Frankfurt/M. (mit Suzanne Wild); **2004** Gallery Kaze, Osaka, kuratiert vom Goethe-Institut Kansai (mit Suzanne Wild); **2000** Galerie Erhard Witzel, Wiesbaden und Museum Goch / Niederrhein (mit Suzanne Wild); **1999** Galerie Bässmann & Cadoz, Düsseldorf; **1998** APT-Gallery, London (mit Suzanne Wild); Standort-Ausstellungshalle e.V., Frankfurt/M.; **1997** Heart Gallery, Mannheim; Galerie Bässmann & Cadoz, Düsseldorf; **1996** Galerie Erhard Witzel, Wiesbaden; Städtische Galerie im Kornhaus, Kirchheim/Teck; **1995** Lichtwerk, Bielefeld (artists unlimited); **1994** Galerie Erhard Witzel, Wiesbaden; **1993** Forum Frankfurter Sparkasse, Frankfurt/M.; **1992** Kommunale Galerie im Leinwandhaus, Frankfurt/M.; **1991** Galerie Erhard Witzel, Wiesbaden; **1989** Galerie Erhard Witzel, Offenbach (mit Kai Bauer und Thomas Schnurr); **1988** SPACEX Gallery, Exeter

Ausstellungsbeteiligungen (Auswahl).: 2013 Galerie Alexandra Erlhoff, Berlin; Galerie Barbara Oberem, Bremen; Institut für Alles Mögliche, Berlin; Kunstverein Neuhausen und Kunstverein Gästezimmer, Stuttgart; **2012** AtelierFrankfurt, Frankfurt/M.; Deutsche Bischofskonferenz, Bonn; Kunstverein Lola Montez, Frankfurt/M.; **2011** Stadtmuseum Simeonstift, Trier und Museum der Brotkultur, Ulm; Musée d'Histoire de la Ville de Luxembourg; **2010** Stamford Works, Dalston, London und The Centre of Creative Collaboration, University of London; **2009** Heinrich-Böll-Stiftung, Berlin; QuadrART Dornbirn; **2008** The National Art Studio Gallery, Changdong, Seoul; Goethe-Institut, Seoul; KNUA Korea National University of Arts, Seoul; Chuncheon Mime Festival (Studio Gallery), Chuncheon; **2006/07** Canal de la Thielle, Le Landeron und Gapcheon Stream, DaeJeon; (in Zusammenarbeit mit dem Metropolitan Museum of Art, DaeJeon); **2006** Musée d'art et d'histoire Neuchâtel; **2004** Museum Goch / Niederrhein; **2005** Heart Gallery, Mannheim; **2001** Neuer Kunstverein Aschaffenburg e.V.; Galerie Erhard Witzel, Wiesbaden; 2000 Kunstverein Eisenturm, Mainz; **1998** Galerie Helmut Pabst, Frankfurt/M.; Kunst-Raum-Akademie, Kloster Weingarten; Galerie Erhard Witzel, Wiesbaden; **1997** Standort-Ausstellungshalle e.V., Frankfurt/M.; Maritime Museum, Vittoriosa, Malta; Galerie Erhard Witzel, Wiesbaden; Galerie Hübner + Hübner, Frankfurt/M.; Schloss Holligen, Bern; **1996** Schmidl & Haas, Frankfurt/M. und Haus am Lützowplatz, Berlin; **1994** Kunstverein Frankfurt/M.; Galerie im Karmeliterkloster Frankfurt/M.; **1993** City Racing, London; **1992** Galerie ak Hans Svorowski, Frankfurt/M.; Raiffeisenhalle Frankfurt/M.; **1991** Galerie im Karmeliterkloster Frankfurt/M.; **1990** Frauenmuseum Bonn und De Beyerd, Breda; Kunstraum Göppingen; Gesellschaft der Freunde Junger Kunst, Baden-Baden; **1989** Musée D'Art Contemporain, Lyon; **1988** Badischer Kunstverein, Karlsruhe.

Arbeiten in folgenden Sammlungen: Sammlung Zeitgenössischer Kunst Deutsche Bank (Frankfurt/M., Leipzig, Wien, Marbella); Graphische Sammlung, Staedel Museum, Frankfurt/M.; Museum Goch / Niederrhein; Sammlung Kulturamt Frankfurt/M.; Hessisches Ministerium für Wissenschaft und Kunst, Wiesbaden; Sammlung der Hypobank München.

Mein besonderer Dank gilt / Special thanks to:
Elisabeth Abendroth, Klaus Benderoth, Wonge Bergmann, Bruno Dorn, Mareike Hennig, Bianka Huber, Sook Jin-Jo, Susanne Kujer, Susanne Lewalter, Eva Mongi-Vollmer, Evangelia Pitsou, Judith Rosenthal, Rose-Lore Scholz, Ray Steel, Nina Trauth, Florence Isabel Wild, Suzanne Wild und Sinje Wobbe

Impressum / Imprint

Herausgeber / editor: Albrecht Wild
Layout / design: Bruno Dorn, Albrecht Wild, Frankfurt/M.
Übersetzung / translation: Judith Rosenthal, Frankfurt/M.
Lektorat / editorial proofreading: Michael Zuch, Frankfurt/M.
Druck / printing: Druckerei Hassmüller, Frankfurt/M.
Fotonachweis: Wenn nicht anders genannt: alle Fotografien © Albrecht Wild / VG Bild-Kunst
Kontakt / contact: wild_albrecht@yahoo.com

bruno dorn verlag, Salzschlirfer Str. 18, D-60386 Frankfurt/M. / Torstraße 37, D-10119 Berlin
www.debook.de . info@debook.de . Telefon 049.69.36 70 75 13

Vertrieb / distribution: bruno dorn verlag, Salzschlirfer Str. 18, D-60386 Frankfurt/M. / Torstraße 37, D-10119 Berlin
www.debook.de . info@debook.de . Telefon 049.69.36 70 75 13

Bibliografische Information der Deutschen Nationalbibliothek: Die Deutsche Nationalbibliothek verzeichnet diese Publikation in der Deutschen Nationalbibliografie; detaillierte bibliografische Daten sind im Internet über http://dnb.d-nb.de abrufbar. / *Bibliographic information published by the Deutsche Nationalbibliothek: The Deutsche Nationalbibliothek lists this publication in the Deutsche Nationalbibliografie; detailed bibliographic data are available in the Internet at http://dnb.d-nb.de.*

Auflage: 800 Exemplare — ISBN 978-3-942311-08-3 — Printed in Germany

Mit freundlicher Unterstützung von / Kindly supported by:

Literaturhaus Villa Clementine

WIESBADEN Kulturamt

HESSEN Hessisches Ministerium für Wissenschaft und Kunst

Stadt Kulturamt Frankfurt am Main

PLOT.COM